What Can Tarot Spells Do for You?

Life is full of uncertainty. We are pushed and pulled by many contending forces; all too often, many of us feel that we are "victims." When we take control of our situation, the world becomes friendly and accommodating rather than harsh and implacable. We gain a competitive edge and a greater sense of security and self-confidence. That is why Janina Renée created *Tarot Spells*.

Performing spells that use strong, positive visualizations and affirmations can help us enhance the quality of our lives and stay focused on our goals. The spells contained in this book are used in conjunction with the Robin Wood Tarot deck. These spells cover a wide variety of common problems and concerns: money, health, family, friends and colleagues, birth and death, marriage and divorce. They are easy to perform, providing a creative support for everyday living.

You don't need to know anything about the Tarot or how to read and interpret the cards. All you need to use *Tarot Spells* is a Tarot deck and a positive and creative frame of mind. The spells and their visualizations and affirmations have genuine psychological value, and provide a pleasant and effective way to steer your life in the direction you want.

About the Author

Janina Renée (Michigan) holds a B.A. degree in anthropology and is working toward a Ph.D. in culture studies. She is a scholar of such diverse subjects as folklore, mythology, ancient religion, psychology, medical anthropology, and American history and literature. As part of her desire to explore means by which to translate the magic and mystery of the old ways into practices that are meaningful for modern people, Janina is currently experimenting with the application of folk magic techniques to problems related to autistic spectrum disorders and other learning disabilities. She is also studying the links between ritualism and nature writing.

To Write to the Author

If you wish to contact the author or would like more information about this book, please write to the author in care of Llewellyn Worldwide and we will forward your request. Both the author and publisher appreciate hearing from you and learning of your enjoyment of this book and how it has helped you. Llewellyn Worldwide cannot guarantee that every letter written to the author can be answered, but all will be forwarded. Please write to:

Janina Renée
‰ Llewellyn Worldwide
2143 Wooddale Drive, Dept. 978-0-87542-670-9
Woodbury, MN 55125-2989, U.S.A.

Please enclose a self-addressed stamped envelope for reply,
or $1.00 to cover costs. If outside U.S.A., enclose
international postal reply coupon.

Many of Llewellyn's authors have websites with additional information and resources. For more information, please visit our website at http://www.llewellyn.com

TAROT SPELLS

Janina Renée

Llewellyn Publications
Woodbury, Minnesota

Revised Edition
Twenty-third Printing, 2007

Revised edition book design and editing by Kimberly Nightingale
Cover photograph © 2000 by Doug Deutscher
Cover design by Anne Marie Garrison
Illustration page 10 by Kerigwen

The Tarot cards used in this book are from *The Robin Wood Tarot* © 1991 by Robin Wood.

Library of Congress Cataloging-in-Publication Data
Renée, Janina
    Tarot Spells / by Janina Renée.
    p.   cm. —
    Includes bibliographical references.
    ISBN 13: 978-0-87542-670-9
    ISBN 10: 0-87542-670-0
    1. Tarot. 2. Magic.   I. Title.   II. Series.

BF1879.T2R46   1990   89–77199
133.3'2424—dc20   CIP

Llewellyn Publications
A Division of Llewellyn Worldwide, Ltd.
2143 Wooddale Drive, Dept. 978-0-87542-670-9
Woodbury, MN 55125-2989, U.S.A.
www.llewellyn.com
Llewellyn is a registered trademark of Llewellyn Worldwide, Ltd.
Printed in the United States of America

Other Books by Janina Renée

By Candlelight (Llewellyn Publications, 2004)
Tarot for a New Generation (Llewellyn Publications, 2001)
Tarot: Your Everyday Guide (Llewellyn Publications, 2000)
Playful Magic (Llewellyn Publications, 1994)

This book is dedicated to
my dad,
whose help with baby sitting in the summer of 1988
enabled me to get it written.

Also, a special acknowledgement
to Ed Fitch,
who let me use him as a sounding board
when I was composing this book.

Contents

The Spells

Artistic and Creative Concerns

Beauty, Health, and Fitness

Business

Change

Children

Competition

Courage

Decisions

Divorce

Dreams

Emotions

Enemies

Families

Farms and Gardens

Friends

Health and Healing

Houses and Homes

Jobs and Job Hunting

Knowledge

Legal Undertakings

Love and Romance

Luck

Money

Motivation

Obstacles

Protection

Psychism

Quarrels

Self-Improvement

Stress

Theft

Appendices

Bibliography

Introduction:
Tarot and the New Age

The Tarot is a series of cards, similar to playing cards, that is best known for its use in fortunetelling. Tarot cards reveal mystical and philosophical truths through their pictures. These symbolic images open the door of the subconscious by drawing from ancient archetypes found deep within our collective subconscious minds. Because the Tarot's psychic and psychological validity has been proven, it is becoming more popular for use in meditation and for other purposes. Today's artists have found special inspiration in the Tarot imagery, so many new versions of these cards have been designed; and the Tarot's increasing popularity is making it widely available.

The Tarot has special uses in magic—the art of "making things happen"—because it enables us to see others and ourselves in an ageless and magical setting. This is especially relevant to what has been called the "New Age." New Age philosophy teaches that as ordinary people we can transform our daily lives and achieve our goals through magical thinking. We can find our own power and break through our limitations by bringing our outer world into harmony with our inner beings and by phrasing our thoughts and actions as positive affirmations.

This book is a new departure on a timeless subject. It presents a way of reaching deep within yourself by using cards and symbols of great antiquity to influence and change the course of events and the world around you. Magical avenues to personal attainment are opened through the use of card layouts, visualizations, meditations, affirmations, and symbolic actions.

Background

The exact origin of the Tarot is uncertain. Scholars who have probed this subject point to the fourteenth and fifteenth centuries as the earliest time during which the existence of the Tarot as we know it can be proven. Eden Gray, author of one of the most popular Tarot textbooks, cites A.D. 1390 as the date of some Tarot cards displayed in a European museum. However, like many other scholars, Gray felt that this particular pack had more ancient antecedents.

The older versions of the Tarot have in their graphics and symbolism a strong medieval Italian feeling, so some scholars, pointing to correspondences in the art and culture of that period, suggest a medieval Italian origin for the Tarot. Many admirers of the Tarot, however, feel that it is far more ancient than that. They differ in their opinion of the Tarot's beginnings. In its motifs they see derivations of the mystical traditions of such varied cultures as ancient Egypt, India, China, Korea, Persia, and that of the Gypsies, as well as Hermetic, Cabalistic, and Albigensian philosophical teachings. Astrological and numerological symbolism has also been projected into the Tarot.

Just as there is dispute over the origin of the Tarot, there are also varying opinions on the meaning of its name. Different scholars believe they have traced its etymology to the aforementioned ancient cultures and religious systems.

Although the historical origins and the meaning of the word "Tarot" cannot be proven, I think we can agree that its motifs are very compelling and correspond to fundamental human psychological experiences.

Tarot Decks

Tarot decks generally take the form of a pack of seventy-eight cards. Twenty-two cards make up the Major Arcana, the more esoteric segment of the Tarot. The symbolic pictures of these cards depict the individual's journey through life, in which he or she undergoes life's lessons to gain experience and achieve self-actualization. The other fifty-six cards, known as the Minor Arcana, are divided into suits (similar to those of playing cards) of fourteen cards each, including the court cards: Kings, Queens, Knights, and Pages. Sometimes they are illustrated, as is the Major Arcana, and sometimes they just have the symbols of their suits: the swords, pentacles, wands, cups, and their variations.

In recent years, the Tarot has blossomed in many versions from an extremely wide diversity of sources. So many decks are currently available that it would not be practical to mention them all here. Some of them hearken back to the early Renaissance versions; others take some interesting new directions.

In 1910, Arthur Edward Waite commissioned a deck that was illustrated by Pamela Colman Smith and printed by Rider (therefore variously known as the Rider-Smith-Waite deck). Prior to that, most of the decks were fairly simple and reflected medieval influences.

Waite altered and/or embellished some of the older Tarot images in the Major Arcana, and ascribed new illustrations and fixed meanings to the Minor Arcana. Waite's deck became very popular, and his illustrations and interpretations became the standard on which many newer Tarot versions have been based. This book utilizes the Tarot deck designed by Robin Wood and published by Llewellyn Publications.

The proliferation of Tarot decks today is like a myriad of performances and interpretations of Shakespeare: all have validity and emotional richness. They call upon similar archetypes, interpreted by a variety of magical philosophers. Many are highly specialized and each individual can, hopefully, find a deck that has personal meaning.

When I first started studying Tarot, I worked mainly with the Waite deck. Later, I switched to the Marseille pack, as I wanted the most historically accurate deck. Nowadays I have my own system of interpretation, which is a synthesis of older and newer interpretations. Since I've come to a point at which feeling is more important to me than form, I no longer insist on authenticity. I recently began a search for a Tarot deck that would really speak to me personally; eventually I chose the Hanson-Roberts deck, which has a dreamy, fairy-tale quality. I feel that those of you who are just getting into Tarot will be pleasantly surprised by the selection available, and that you'll be able to experiment with a number of fascinating decks in your exploration of the magic that is implicit in every card.

Tarot Applications

For centuries, the Tarot has been used to foresee the patterns of the future. For Tarot readings, the cards are shuffled and then laid out in certain traditional spreads. Interpreting the symbols in relation to the questions asked projects the future. Similarly, the cards can be shuffled, laid out, and studied to show the individual's place in terms of spiritual development as well as in the grand scheme of life.

Tarot also has unique value as a tool for meditation. By reflecting on the deep meanings of the symbols, the individual can look inward to probe truths about the Self, or look outward to grasp transcendental cosmic knowledge.

Today, the magic of the Tarot is also being enthusiastically explored. Practitioners are developing psychic and psychological exercises to encourage self-knowledge, healing, creativity, etc. Indeed, the Tarot has been worked into systems of "high magic," that is, rituals for higher spiritual transformation. Truly, the use of the Tarot has been expanded, from a means of sensing patterns and events to a forthright method of influencing our own evolution.

About the Spells in This Book

In this book, I have endeavored to link the archaic art and power of the Tarot to a simple and effective means of achieving personal goals. The spells in this book are slanted to "getting things done," especially in the mundane world about us. The material environment we live in takes work and adaptation as we make our ways through it. The stresses of modern life seem to demand 90 percent of our thoughts, emotions, and efforts, so we must be able to meet these demands in any way possible. The Tarot spells provided here offer such a way. Yet, behind all of the actions, visualizations, meditations, and affirmations in these spells are the deeper and more profound spiritual and psychological values of the Tarot.

Although Tarot cards are used as the focus of each of these spells, many of them can be enhanced by other magical methods:

* The art of creative visualization has been recognized as a new form of magic, and the spells here call for visualizations in connection with the placing of the cards. In the visualizations, the desired goals are imaged as being carried out and completed.

* Symbolic actions, motions, and gestures are also sometimes called for in a type of "imitative magic": the art of dramatizing the course of action you want taken.

* All of the spells use positive affirmations, based on the occult belief that when you say a thing is true, it is true.

* Other techniques, drawn from metaphysical philosophy as well as folk magic, are used as well. There are also methods of enhancing the spells through the use of the magic of candles, color, crystals, and other accessories, enabling you to focus more clearly on your goals and to magnify the magic that is sent forth.

Although all this may seem rather complicated, the spells are designed to be fairly simple, and you have the option to embellish them as you desire.

How Tarot Magic Works

The Tarot deck, with all its many variations, uses a highly evocative symbolic language. These symbols, speaking directly to our unconscious minds, can create a strong emotional response. When used in combinations, these symbols can be used to make complex statements. Although the Tarot has long been valued as a tool for meditation and divination, the Tarot symbolism can also be used as a focal point for working magic. With this method, the cards are arranged deliberately to state the goal that the user wants to achieve.

Tarot Spells Are Easy

You don't need any previous knowledge of the Tarot or ability with Tarot divination to work the spells provided in this book. Just go through your deck until you find the cards that the individual spells require, and then arrange them as the layouts indicate.

Magic

There are, of course, many definitions of what magic is and how it works. That which we call magic can be divided into two categories: "high magic," which is worked to bring about spiritual and metaphysical transformations within the individual, and the more familiar sort of magic which is used to achieve certain desires and goals. This book concerns itself more with pragmatic spells that address everyday concerns—romance, family matters, job concerns, legal problems, and so on. However, there are also spells for working toward personal betterment, and it will be found that working with the rich symbolism of the Tarot will have an uplifting effect.

Magic and Probability

For the purposes of the practical spells in this book, a useful working definition of magic is "using the power of the mind to nudge probabilities." By influencing probabilities, you can encourage circumstances to develop in your favor.

Because there are numerous factors that influence the course of our daily lives, there are multiple probabilities for the directions that our lives, as well as circumstances in general, can take. Among the things that can influence the shaping of events are conscious and unconscious thoughts. Some occultists believe in the existence of an ethereal "plane of thought," where ideas can take on a type of reality that serves as a template for actions and occurrences on the physical plane (i.e., in the real world). It is also believed that our unconscious minds can communicate directly to the unconscious minds of other persons, thus influencing their thoughts and actions.

The magic worker can therefore use his or her will to impose a template on the plane of thought, or to send messages to the unconscious minds of others.

The Tarot spells provided here will serve as a means for you to focus your will and communicate your desires to your own subconscious, the minds of others, and to the Plane of Thought in the language of the unconscious mind—the language of symbolism. (In fact, even if you don't believe in magic, you can accept that focusing on these symbols can help you achieve a frame of mind that will bring about greater self-confidence and success.)

Of course, if you want to use mental power to bring about an event that is fairly well within the realm of probability, you stand a better chance of succeeding than if you want something to occur that is unlikely. A skilled magic user is sensitive to the natural flow of events and the forces that affect circumstances, and is thus able to determine how to most easily influence these events by utilizing the best possibilities for changing them.

Practical example: You can use some of the magical spells in this book to create a very favorable feeling toward yourself in the subconscious mind of a potential employer. If you and the other applicants who are contending for the job are all equally skilled and qualified, the employer's unconscious bias can be turned toward you, increasing the probability that you will be chosen. However, if you are not truly qualified for the job, this obvious fact will cause the employer's rational mind to override the bias, and the probability that you will be chosen will become very slim despite your attempts to influence the decision.

Ethics

With the use of magic, the question of ethics arises. When using these spells, bear in mind that:

* We can plant suggestions to get others to react favorably toward us, however, we cannot turn them into our slaves. As it is, a spell to influence a person has a better chance of succeeding if you activate a thought that was already in that person's mind; it has less of a chance if you try to plant a thought that is repugnant to that person.

* The use of magic does not necessarily give you an "unfair" edge over other people, as our lives are affected by so many capricious and random factors. Fate does not hand out privileges equally, and all sorts of irrational biases, prejudices, and bits of misinformation influence the decisions of people in power over us. Magic can be seen as just another variable to be thrown into this whole cauldron of circumstance, which hopefully will bring a little extra luck to help things go your way.

* Thoughts have vibrations, and so your mental state influences the energy field around you. If you use negative, harmful spells, you are necessarily projecting negative emotions. These emotions will cling to you and act in a magnetic way to attract "bad luck." The opposite principle works when you use spells to do good. As the African proverb goes, "wish evil to no man, for the perpetrator of good sees good, and the perpetrator of evil sees evil."

* Among spiritual people, it is a common belief that all individuals possess a "Higher Self" or "Soul-Self" or other guardian power that forms a connection with the Divine, urging them to do good, and looking out for their best interests. (In Ceremonial Magic, these concepts are

combined in the idea of the Holy Guardian Angel.)
Unfortunately, many people are not in clear communication
with their Higher Selves, otherwise there would be no crime
nor cruelty in the world. However, spells and rituals that
prod a person to "do the right thing" have more power
because they speak directly to a person's soul, and actually
send energy that helps to empower that person's Soul-Self.
On the other hand, rituals to harm an innocent person will
provoke resistance and backlash.

For the purposes of this book, spells are designed to be as positive as possible, even when they deal with something negative. For example, the spells to counteract enemies are designed to restrain them and keep them away, but not to hurt them. The layouts have no cards with very negative associations, except where they are truly pertinent to make the necessary statement. The spells are phrased in such a way as to focus on the positive aspects of any situation.

How to Work the Tarot Spells

In these spells, the cards are arranged so that the pictures make a meaningful statement. The shapes of the layouts also tend to be significant. For each spell, the meanings of the cards and layouts used are explained and other instructions for working the spells are given, including magical visualizations to go with each spell.

Generally, the spells are designed to help the subject achieve some goal. The subject is the person a given spell focuses on. If you are doing the spells to help yourself, then you are "the subject." However, the subject can also be someone on whose behalf you are performing the spell or someone that you are trying to influence. Also, some spells have institutions, other entities, or even abstract concepts as subjects. In Tarot readings, the subject is most commonly known as "the Significator." Many spells will call for a card to represent the subject or Significator. Refer to appendix I for a list of cards, which can be used as Significators.

For consistency, most of the spells are written with the assumption that you, the person doing the spell, are working the spell for yourself, that you are the subject, and that you will be using your own Significator where called for in the layouts, unless otherwise noted. If you want to perform a spell on behalf of someone else, use that person in the visualization, change the wording of the affirmation to include that person's name, and make other changes where necessary.

Card Meanings

These spells were originally designed using the "Rider-Waite" deck (sometimes called the "Pamela Colman Smith" deck). The illustrations in this book, however, use the Robin Wood Tarot deck. I have admired Robin's work in other Llewellyn publications, and felt that since the structure is similar to the Waite deck, and magical in concept, it would be appropriate here.

The Robin Wood deck was both designed and drawn by Robin Wood. It is based in part on earlier decks, and employs pagan symbols and traditional meanings that can be traced back to medieval times and that have their roots in far more ancient cultures. If you happen to have a Tarot deck that you favor and prefer not to use either the Waite or the Wood deck, you shouldn't have any problems with most of these spells. Occasionally, some spells will be designed so that the figures in the pictures face each other or are pointing to each other. If this is the case, you should check your cards to make sure that the figures are facing the same way. If they aren't, try to switch them around to see if they can be made to face each other.

For cards used in these spells, I tend to use the basic interpretations as set forth by Waite, and occasionally some of the other traditional interpretations. I emphasize the meanings that I've found most applicable in my many years of card-reading experience. It should be noted that even with standard interpretations:

* Some cards can have multiple meanings. For example, the Lovers can in some cases refer to physical or romantic love between two individuals; it can also signify an individual's need to choose between two conflicting courses of action. Another example: depending upon the circumstances, the chariot can refer to travel, news, victory and conquest, or control over conflicting forces.

* The symbolism of some cards can take on special meanings for certain individuals. In other words, the "feeling" that an individual has for certain cards can be important.

* With some of these spells, certain aspects of the artwork in a card can take on importance. For example: the Moon is generally a card standing for emotions as well as for the mysteries of the subconscious mind. However, in the section

on spells done for the benefit of animals, the Moon is one of the cards suggested for use as a significator for dogs, since dogs are depicted in the artwork and there are no cards in the Tarot specifically designated to represent pets.

* The way figures in the cards are posed is significant to some of the spells. As an example, in spells that seek to bring forth secrets or hidden information, the Hermit, representing discovery, is placed to the right of the High Priestess, representing secrets, so that the Hermit's lamp is held up pointing to the High Priestess.

You can see that the possible meanings for some cards go on and on—but you can also see that there's a common thread of interpretation running through the Tarot. Generally, the symbols on the cards speak for themselves in the context of the spells for which they are used. Of course, clarification and extra information will be provided.

Use of Cards

Throughout these spells, I use cards that tend to be strong and positive. Thus you'll notice that cards such as the Sun, the World, Temperance, and the Star are used over and over again— they're just such powerful, lucky cards! Negative cards such as the Devil are used very seldom, and only when it's necessary to explain a particular situation.

Sometimes Tarot books will provide explanations for inverted cards. However, inverted cards are seldom used in these spells, because their meanings tend to be more ambiguous and because the cards in their regular positions are designed to cover a wide scope of meanings.

Layout of Cards

The cards in these spells are laid out in patterns that are meaningful and easy to concentrate on. One of the most frequently used layouts is the three-card spread. This pattern is very good for making a concise statement of the goal to be achieved, and it is easy for the eye to focus on and the mind to remember. Depending upon the situation, the cards in the three-card spread can be used to designate:

* Subject—Action necessary—Object desired.

* Past—Present—Future.

* First event—Second event—Third event.

* Initial action—Progress—Outcome.

* Influence—Subject—Influence.

Layouts can also take the form of protective crosses, pyramids showing the ascent of a matter, or inverted pyramids showing the descent of a matter, steps leading upward or downward, etc. The illustrations will show you how to arrange the cards, and wherever the layouts are of particular significance, explanations will be given.

Accessories for Spells

Some of the spells in this book require special accessories that enhance the spell by helping to focus its power on the desired objective.

Generally, these accessories are easily obtainable; for example, a spell may call for a mirror, or a knife, or a goblet, or candles of a certain color, etc. With most of the spells, however, accessories are entirely optional. It's your choice if you want to embellish them. If you like, you may arrange things such as flowers, candles, crystals, gemstones, etc., to act simply as decorations for enhancing the area where you plan to lay out the cards and perform the spells. Or, you may want to step up the power and sharpen the focus of your spells by using these accessories as effective magical tools.

Each of the various spells will list what sort of accessories are needed or could be useful. For more information on these magical tools, refer to the appendices, which cover special preparations for spells and accessories including candles, crystals, and color correspondences and their significance in magic.

Action

Some of the spells ask you to perform certain actions. For example, you may be asked to write things on paper, or inscribe names on candles, or pour water in and out of goblets, or bury or hide things at the four corners of your property, or seal things in jars, etc. None of the actions required will be difficult or preposterous. Such actions may be required either before performing a spell, during the visualizations or affirmations, or after completing the spell.

Meditation and Visualization

Each spell has a meditation/visualization that is done when the individual cards are laid out. Most of these visualizations are built around the traditional or graphic meanings of the cards as applied to your personal situation. You will be asked to concentrate on visualizing these images or to sense certain feelings very strongly, as if the events detailed were unfolding in front of you.

Affirmations

Each spell provides affirmations, which are highly positive and phrased in the present tense. Typical affirmations read "I have . . . " rather than "I will have . . . ," because within the framework of magical reality, if you say a thing is true, it is true. Many of these affirmations can be used to enhance daily positive thinking, even when you aren't performing the spells.

After Completing a Spell

Until your purpose is accomplished, you may leave your arrangement in place, if convenient. If you want to reinforce the power of your spell, you may pause by your card arrangement for a few moments each day. If you have time, you can light incense and candles, touch each card as you say its significance, and then put out the candles. If it is not convenient for you to leave your card patterns out, just clean everything up and put all your accessories away; the spell will go on working.

Do not think about your spell once you have performed it, and be careful not to dwell on or brood over the thing that your spell seeks to accomplish during your waking hours. Magic works best when it is entirely given over to the unconscious mind and the spiritual powers.

If you are able, you may use your cards as amulets by carrying them around with you in your purse or briefcase. When you want to use your cards for some new purpose, take them (the cards you used in the spell) out under the moonlight and wipe them off with a clean cloth. If your cards are plastic-coated, wipe them off with a cloth that has been dampened with water mixed with sea salt.

To perform the Tarot spells, it is not necessary to perform a ritual. Simply laying out the designated cards and meditating on them can be enough. However, for most people it is very helpful to use a ritual in performing the magic of the Tarot. The following rite gives you a format for shaping and channeling your subconscious mind to best accomplish such work. Eventually you might want to modify and abridge this ritual, or devise rituals of your own, as you become more accustomed to placing yourself into a magical state of mind.

Rite for Tarot Magic

Arrange for some time to be alone and undisturbed; an hour would be about right. If you have music available, put on something that is calm, serene, and meditative. Take a relaxing bath, imagining strongly that you are cleansing not only your body, but also your soul and spirit as well. Dress in costume, or wear jewelry that has a particularly "magical" feel for you.

You will need a clean, flat surface to use as an altar to lay out the cards for your spell. An out-of-the-way table or dresser top that will remain undisturbed for as long as you need it will do.

The accompanying illustration on page ten gives an example of how you could set up a Tarot card spell with cards and accessories. Set out an incense burner, two or more candles (with colors appropriate to the work you are doing, as suggested in the individual spells), your Tarot deck, and this book (plus two bookmarks to mark this ritual and the spell you will be using). Other magical implements may be suggested in conjunction with various spells. You may also make your arrangement more elaborate by setting out flowers, crystals or gemstones, and by using colored cloths on which to lay everything.

When all is in readiness, pause for a silent meditation, placing your mind in a serene, receptive state. Hold this quiet, contemplative state for as long as seems appropriate. Then light the candles. Now hold your hands over the layout in an attitude of invocation or blessing and say these or similar words:

1. Rite for Tarot magic with accessories.

Invocation

"I call now upon the Earth,
far plains and lofty mountains,
for power and strength to my spell,
as I light this candle in summoning.

"I call now upon the waters,
broad lakes, ever-moving streams,
and the boundless ocean,
for power and strength to my spell,
as I light this candle in summoning.

"I call now upon the skies,
the four winds of Earth,
and the far reaches of infinite spaces,
for power and strength to my spell,
as I light this candle in summoning.

"I call now upon the deep fires
that burn in the core of the Earth,
at one with the energies of life itself,
for power and strength to my spell
as I light this candle in summoning."

Pause for the length of five heartbeats, then pick up the Tarot deck and remove the significant cards for your spell, saying in these or similar words:

"Reaching far into the archaic past
I draw forth these symbols
to shape the spell I cast.
Here shall be woven chance, fortune, and fate
that my deepest wish may be
swiftly attained."

At this point, turn to the specific spell you wish to perform and lay the cards out according to the diagram provided. Use the visualizations provided as you lay out each card.

After you have laid out the cards and made the appropriate meditations and visualizations, carefully and with as much feeling as you can, read aloud the affirmation provided by the spell for the subject of your magic.

To close this rite, you may add more incense to the burner, and summarize in your own words the matter that you are working to accomplish. Once again, consider the cards and visualize the event as happening. Do this for a period of at least twenty-five heartbeats. Time is not as important here as is the complete and total concentration on that which you wish to accomplish. Do it, and do it well!

Then hold your hands out over the cards, as if to charge them with the Power that you visualize being drawn through your entire body and out through your hands, as you say in these or similar words:

Affirmation

"Into these cards, I direct great powers!
Power drawn from within me,
and power called from those spiritual forces
which are at work around me.
O wide-ruling powers
mark well what I have done here,
and work to make it manifest!
So shall it be!"

"I call upon you, O beings of nature . . .
of plains and mountains, of oceans and lakes,
of far deserts, deep forests, and distant tundra.

Of the heart of the planet itself.
Mark well what I have done here,
and work to make it manifest!
So shall it be!

"I place my petition before you,
O Earth, giver of all life,
and Sky, thou who art infinite and eternal.
May you lend strength and power
to this, my spell!
So shall it be!"

Remain before your card arrangement for a period of at least twenty-five heart-beats, contemplating the cards and visualizing the subject of your spell as being accomplished. Put all of the candles out. Then kiss your hand in salute or render some other such salute to the Powers, and depart.

The Spells

Action

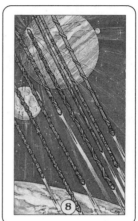

2. To get action and/or set forces in motion.

*T*his layout may be seen as a staircase leading upward. The Ace of Wands stands for the active principle—forces set in motion. The Chariot stands for forces which are in motion and under control. The Eight of Wands shows movement toward a goal.

If you wish to use accessories for this spell, red candles, red flowers, reddish crystals and gemstones, and a red cloth on which to lay the cards are appropriate, as red is a color representing action and vitality.

The ritual for this spell can be performed at anytime, although the most appropriate time would be first thing in the morning, especially on a day that you feel is a good day for new action or new beginnings.

To perform this spell, you may use the ritual provided in chapter 1, improvise a ritual of your own, or just proceed by laying out the cards and doing the following meditation, visualization, and affirmation.

Meditation and Visualization

Lay out the cards when you come to the appropriate point in the spell.

Since this spell is designed to be a general-purpose rite adapted to a great variety of uses, I can't give very detailed visualization suggestions for it. However, the following general visualization will be useful.

As you lay down the Ace of Wands, visualize the early stages of action or chain of events that you wish to set in motion.

As you lay down the Chariot, visualize these actions or events developing in an orderly manner.

Finally, as you lay down the Eight of Wands, visualize your desires accelerating toward their ultimate goal.

Note: If you wish to employ a more symbolic visualization, you can use the Chariot as your focal point, visualizing a chariot drawn by horses racing toward a goal. The horses have fiery eyes and run on air, with sparks flying from their hooves. You can also visualize this image being superimposed over the aforementioned images.

At the appropriate point in the ritual, after your visualization, recite the following affirmation.

Affirmation

"I call upon the power that is within me!
I call upon those wide-ranging powers
that are at work in the universe around me!
I charge these powers all
that my desire be fulfilled.
Forces are set in motion!
Circumstances are shaped!
Activity commences!
Events unfold!
Deeds are accomplished!
All is resolved in my favor!
The magical momentum that I have built
continues to build rapidly,
and all that I wish is attained!
So be it!"

You may consider the spell closed at this point, or you may close the spell as suggested in the rite in chapter 1, or as desired.

Significator

3. To stimulate a particular person to "get going."

*T*his is a spell that you would most likely use when a particular person has been putting off doing something or has not been able to find the motivation to get started on something that is important.

This layout can be seen as an arrow directed at the person who is the subject of this spell. As in the previous spell, the Ace of Wands, Chariot, and the Eight of Wands used together denote forces being activated. The top card represents the person who needs to take action. To choose a card to stand for the individual in question, refer to the section on Significators beginning on page 4 or appendix 1, or use the Magician. The Magician is an appropriate Significator card for this spell, because it depicts an individual taking action, as well as acting upon his or her surroundings.

As in the previous spell, accessories such as red candles, flowers, crystals and gemstones, and red cloths on which to lay the cards, will all suggest the energy and vitality which you desire to raise. If you have a picture or some belonging of the subject, include this on or near the altar arrangement to help you focus on this individual.

The ritual for this spell can be performed at anytime, although first thing in the morning is most appropriate—especially on a day that you feel is a good one for new action or new beginnings.

To work this spell, you may use the ritual provided in chapter 1, improvise a ritual of your own, or just proceed by laying out the cards and doing the following meditation, visualization, and affirmation.

Meditation and Visualization

Lay out the cards when you come to the appropriate point in the spell.

For this spell, you will need to visualize the person in question taking the necessary action, or doing whatever it is that he or she should be doing.

As you lay down the Significator card, visualize this person cloaked in a bright red aura and full of energy and enthusiasm to tackle whatever tasks lie ahead. If you have a picture or some belonging of the subject, you may stroke it while continuing to do this visualization.

As you lay down the Ace of Wands, visualize the early stages of action or chain of events that you wish to set in motion. As you lay down the Chariot, visualize these actions or events developing in an orderly manner.

Finally, as you lay down the Eight of Wands, visualize your desires accelerating toward their ultimate goal.

Affirmation

"This person (name),

is pushed forward to accomplish

that which needs to be done!

Powers from within and without

fill him/her with energy and enthusiasm

to complete this action!

The power and strength grows with him/her

such that action leads to more action

and success leads to more success!

He/she learns the satisfaction

of moving rapidly toward a goal,

gaining more and more magical momentum,

more energy as he/she moves forward!

Leading ultimately to the goals

that I have visualized here.

So be it!"

You may consider the spell closed at this point, or you may close the spell as suggested in the rite in chapter 1.

To get an institution, corporation, or organization moving, use the same layout as number three, but instead of a Significator card representing an individual, use a card representing the institution. (You can substitute or combine this with a calling card or ad with the corporate or organizational logo. Refer to appendix 1 for a list of Significator cards that can be used to represent groups or organizations.)

Addiction

4. For help in overcoming an addiction or bad habit.

*T*his is a layout designed to help in overcoming addictions or habits that are particularly harmful. You can use it to help yourself if you have need, or you can use as the subject another person who needs help. (If doing this spell for another person, alter the meditation and affirmation accordingly.) I do stress that for particularly harmful addictions it is necessary to also seek professional help so that psychology or medicine can also be utilized to break the dependence or habit.

This layout takes the form of an "x" or St. Andrew's cross, symbolizing harmony and the balance of elements that is needed to restore an individual to self-control and wholeness.

In this layout, Strength stands for the ability to overcome problems with the use of willpower. Temperance also stands for willpower in avoiding things and living life in harmonious balance. Judgement stands for breaking free of the habit and making a major self-improvement/transformation. The World stands for wholeness, satisfaction, health, perfection, and happiness.

If you wish to use accessories for this spell, use white candles, flowers, crystals, gemstones, and cloth if you want to emphasize "purification" and "purity" to be attained. If you prefer to emphasize the healing aspects of this spell, however, use the color green.

The ritual for this spell can be performed at anytime. If performing this spell for yourself, it will be especially effective if repeated first thing in the morning and again before going to bed at night. If yours is a particularly strong addiction, be prepared to repeat this spell over and over again until you are satisfied that you have finally conquered the problem.

Mental and emotional factors are important in setting up this ritual. Before performing the rite, meditate on purification while taking a bath (see appendix 2: "Preparation for Spells"), and be sure that you have had plenty of time to think over your resolve to break your habit.

To perform this spell, you may use the ritual provided in chapter 1, improvise a ritual of your own, or just proceed by laying out the cards and doing the following meditation, visualization, and affirmation.

Meditation and Visualization

Lay out the cards when you come to the appropriate point in the spell.

As you lay down the Temperance card, picture a good guardian spirit standing beside you (or the person for whose benefit you are doing this spell), ready to give help and comfort. The angel's great wings spread in a protective manner. Look at the illustration on the Temperance card and consider how it also represents harmony and balance—the balance in life that you need to restore to a life that has been out of kilter. Picture yourself enjoying a life with all forces of body and mind in perfect balance. Imagine the sensation you (or your subject) will feel as refreshing and rejuvenating power surges through the body, restoring wholeness.

As you lay down the Strength card, picture again the ideal you—strong and with the power to withstand all temptation.

Lay down the Judgement card, concentrating on renewal and awakening to a new life. Visualize yourself waking up from a long slumber to find a rejuvenated mind and body, ready to meet all challenges.

Lay down the World. Visualize yourself filled with the joy of life, dancing, singing, and greeting each new day with enthusiasm. Realize that all the powers that you need for success and happiness are to be found within you.

After you have finished meditating on the cards and visualizations, carefully, and with as much feeling as you can, recite the following affirmation.

Affirmation

"With these cards,
and with this spell
power is drawn,
and power surges through me!
By the power within me
I break the chains that bind me!
I break the bonds

which tie my soul and spirit!

I restore my life to balance!

I am resilient!

I can withstand all that comes my way!

For strength is mine,

and I grow stronger

and ever yet stronger than before.

By all the powers that be,

I overcome!"

You may consider the spell closed at this point, or you may close the spell as suggested in chapter 1, or as desired.

Animals

Significator

5. For help in finding a good home for an animal.

*T*he Tarot deck doesn't actually have any cards specifically pertaining to animals. Many decks, however, use animals as symbols in some of the illustrations. For spells involving animals, we can use these cards, concentrating on the animal in the picture and ignoring the card's conventional meaning. In the Waite-Smith deck and some of its variants, cards that can be used as Significators for animals include the Nine of Pentacles, the Star, and the Ace of Cups for birds; the Queen of Wands for cats; Strength for domestic cats and big cats like lions and tigers; the Moon, the Fool, and the Ten of Pentacles for dogs and wolves; the Page of Cups and the Moon for fish and aquatic life; the Sun, the Six of Wands, and all of the Knights for horses; the King of Wands for lizards and reptiles; the Queen of Pentacles for rabbits; and the Lovers for snakes. If you are using another deck, you will want to look it over to see whether it uses the same animal symbols as Waite, and also whether it has other cards that feature animals. If you don't find the above-mentioned possible Significator cards satisfactory, you can also use a picture of the animal or animals in place of a Tarot card to be the Significator.

The squarish, almost solid layout of this spell suggests the four cornerstones of a house. The World represents ideal environmental conditions, the Three of Cups stands for abundance, the Ten of Cups is for a happy family life, and the Four of Wands is "a haven of refuge." Superimposed over these four cards is the animal's Significator card, or a picture of the animal in question.

If you wish to use accessories for this rite, then pink—the color of affectionate love—can be used for candles, flowers, crystals and gemstones, and cloth. You can also have laid out pictures of the animal or animals in question, as well as pieces of hair, feathers, whiskers, etc.

To perform this spell, you may use the ritual provided in chapter 1, improvise a ritual of your own, or just proceed by laying out the cards and doing the following meditation, visualization, and affirmation.

Meditation and Visualization

Lay out the cards when you come to the appropriate point in the spell. Lay down the World, visualizing the ideal type of home you would like to see your pet living in.

As you lay down the Three of Cups, imagine your pet with a new family, enjoying him or herself, having fun participating in all of the activities of this new family, and having everything he or she wants.

Lay down the Ten of Cups, imagining how much you want your pet to love and be loved by this new family. Lay down the Four of Wands, again visualizing a secure and happy home life for your pet.

Finally, lay down the Significator card or photo, again think on your pet and how you want the best of everything for him or her.

After you have finished meditating on the cards and visualizations, carefully, and with as much feeling as you can, recite the following affirmation.

Affirmation

"I call upon all good spirits
and all friendly forces
who care about the well-being
of small and helpless animals!
A new home and a new family
are made available
for my small friend, my pet.
A place of love . . .
A place of happiness . . .
Their love is as my love!
I do not cease from looking
for the new home.
I seek out a place
that happily accepts
my pet, (name),
And he/she is happy there
for the rest of his/her days.
So be it!"

You may consider the spell closed at this point, or you may close the spell as suggested in chapter 1, or as desired.

✳

The Star

1 The Magician 1

Significator

The Hermit

6. For help in finding a lost animal or animals.

*T*his layout is cross-shaped, as the cross is an ancient symbol of protection appropriate for the protective feelings many of us have toward animals, and especially the concern we feel for lost animals. The Six of Cups, which forms the base of this cross, is a card which rekindles love and renews old ties, acting to draw the lost animal back to its home and to the people who love it. The Magician stands for the utilization of resources, and assures that all measures will be taken and all efforts utilized in the search. The Star brings luck and hope—elements very necessary to such an undertaking. The Hermit reveals where that which is lost may be found. Here, the Hermit shines his lamp on the card chosen to represent the lost pet.

If you wish to use accessories for this spell, use pink candles, flowers, crystals, gemstones, and cloth, as pink is the color of affectionate love. If possible, also have some pictures of the missing pet laid out. (You can also include pieces of hair, feathers, whiskers, or such from the pet in question.) Also, for this particular spell you will need to have a lit candle nearby, whether or not you choose to include lighting candles as part of the ritual.

To perform this spell, you may use the ritual provided in chapter 1, improvise a ritual of your own, or just proceed by laying out the cards and doing the following meditation, visualization, and affirmation.

Meditation and Visualization

Lay out the cards when you come to the appropriate point in the spell.

Lay the animal's Significator down first. Visualize the animal, recalling its features and mannerisms to the best of your ability. Picture the missing pet being drawn home to the light of the candles—to the light of love. Hold your hands above the candle flames for a few moments. Feel the warmth of the candles, and visualize the light of the candles acting as a beacon to lead the animal home.

Lay down the Six of Cups, and think about all of the good times you and your pet have had together. Try to remember the day you first got your pet, what he or she was like as a youngster, etc. As you lay down the Magician, consider the various courses of action that may be taken in the search for your pet. Lay down the Star, a card for wishing. Make a wish for your pet to return.

Finally, lay down the Hermit, visualizing your pet being found or returned, and how happy you both will be to be reunited! After you have finished meditating on the cards and visualizations, carefully, and with as much feeling as you can, recite the following affirmation.

Affirmation

"As I set forth these cards
in the light of these candles,
the small friend for whom I have so much love
is drawn home to me!
I do not cease trying to find my friend
until he/she returns home.
I call upon all good spirits
and all good powers
who care about small and helpless creatures
to aid me in my search!
My small friend, (name)
is brought home
through the spell which I call forth.
It shines like a beacon
that my animal friend can see!
So be it!"

You may consider the spell closed at this point, or you may close the spell as suggested in the rite in chapter 1, or as desired.

7. For the protection of threatened or endangered animals.

*T*his layout takes the form of a cross, an ancient symbol of protection. The Moon, which is the focal card, can represent wildlife and wilderness, and all things that live in the primal state of nature. Ironically, the Moon is also a warning of danger. The Star, at the base of the figure, promises help and protection from higher sources. Strength is also a card of protection. Temperance, crowning the cross, represents wise ecological management. The Nine of Wands is a card of protection and defense.

For this spell, you will need to have at least one lit candle. If you wish to use other accessories, you may use green leaves, crystals and gemstones, and cloth. It is good to use the color green for these accessories, as green symbolizes the freedom of nature. Colors typical of the particular elements that the animals live in could also be used; for example, watery blues and greens for sea mammals, fish and aquatic life; deep green for forest animals; appropriate earth tones for desert animals; sky blue for birds, and so on. As another possibility, you could choose colors characteristic of the particular species you are concerned with. Pictures of the type of animal or animals you are concerned about protecting will also be helpful.

To perform this spell, you may use the ritual provided in chapter 1, improvise a ritual of your own, or just proceed by laying out the cards and doing the following meditation, visualization, and affirmation.

Meditation and Visualization

Light the candle, then lay out the cards when you come to the appropriate point in the spell.

First, set down the Moon, visualizing the realm of nature and all its denizens. Now, visualize the particular species you have chosen to help with this spell, making in your mind a picture of those particular animals within their customary habitat.

Next, lay down the Star as you lay down this card, and think of all of the unseen but powerful forces at play in the universe around us. Think of these forces acting together to help those creatures of nature that are so in need of special help.

Set down the Strength card, imagining the protective strength that will be needed in the subject animal's fight for survival.

Lay down the Temperance card, envisioning the guardian angel as the protective spirit that watches over the Earth. Visualize that guardian spirit becoming a special tutelary spirit for the type of animal in question, even visualizing that spirit taking on some of the attributes of that animal. Think also about the special environmental action that may be needed to assure the survival of the subject animals.

Finally, lay down the Nine of Wands. Visualize all forces—human agencies as well as powers natural and supernatural—alerted and ready to protect the endangered animals.

After you have laid down all the cards and done the visualization, hold your hands over the candle flame or flames, make a clockwise circular motion over the candle with your hands, and visualize the candle flames growing to build a warm and protective cone of energy around the animals in question. As you continue, image in your mind—very vividly—that as you build this spell, the field of protection spreads over the face of the Earth, glowing and growing about all of the animals with which the spell is concerned. After you have finished meditating on the cards and visualizations, carefully, and with as much feeling as you can, recite the following affirmation.

Affirmation

"I call upon the mighty forces of Nature!

I call upon all good protective spirits!

The forces of the Earth, and of the waters,

and of the air,

Hear me now!

Help me now!

Lend the power to protect this life form

that is so endangered!

The vast forces,

the power and the energy

which I call forth

grow and redouble!

These animals, the (name)

are aided and protected

and they grow ever more numerous

and ever stronger!

These animals, the (name)

are ever more able to thrive
in the world as it is now,
and the world as it will be in the future!
So be it!"

You may consider the spell closed at this point, or you may close the spell as desired.

Note: If you wish to amend the spell to put more emphasis on help from the government or other establishments in power, substitute the Emperor for the Nine of Wands, and visualize the government or other authority taking action at that point in the ritual.

**Owner's
Significator**

**Animal's
Significator**

8. To encourage an individual owner to take better care of his or her animal(s).

*I*f you are a caring person who is concerned about the well-being of animals, this is a spell that you would most likely want to use when you have reason to believe that a certain owner isn't taking proper care of his or her pets.

Here, Temperance stands for better management and care on the part of the owner. The Three of Cups and Four of Wands are cards representing happiness, playfulness, freedom from want, as well as a happy and secure home and haven of refuge—the home that the animal should have and that the owner should provide.

Note: You may be able to combine the two Significators, as in the Queen of Wands and her cat, or the Fool and his dog. If so, then have the Significator in the center of the bottom row and substitute the Star, for good influences, in the top row.)

If you wish to use accessories for this spell, green candles, crystals and gemstones, and cloth will be helpful to emphasize soothing in a case where an owner has been too rough with his/her pet. Otherwise, pink for affection or white for purity of intentions can work as colors for accessories. A picture of the irresponsible owner and his/her animal or animals will also be a very helpful addition to this spell, though admittedly these may be difficult to obtain. Otherwise fur, hair, or even a rock from the individual's residence can be laid down near the cards to help build a connection for the spell.

To perform this spell, you may use the ritual provided in chapter 1, improvise a ritual of your own, or just proceed by laying out the cards and doing the following meditation, visualization, and affirmation.

Meditation and Visualization

Lay out the cards when you come to the appropriate point in the spell.

First, lay down the owner's Significator card, followed by Temperance. As you do this, visualize this person giving affection and proper care to his or her animal. In your mind's eye, picture the individual as he or she looks currently, and then image him/her taking on the attributes of the good angel in Temperance. Picture him or her changed into a warm and nurturing person.

Next, lay down the Four of Wands, the animal's Significator, and the Three of Cups in turn. Picture the animal in ideal surroundings—those that are loving, secure, and able to meet all of their needs. Also, if changes need to be made in the owner's home or property to better accommodate the animals, visualize these transformations taking place.

After you have finished meditating on the cards and visualizations, carefully, and with as much feeling as you can, recite the following affirmation.

Affirmation

"(Owner's name) comes to realize
that he/she must provide a better home
for his/her pet, (pet's name).
A home with love, and warmth, and proper care,
and in return, his/her pet
returns that kindness threefold.
This spell gives constant urging to the owner,
to improve his/her ways
and continues until the work is accomplished!
So be it!"

You may consider the spell closed at this point, or you may close the spell as desired.

Owner's
Significator

Animal's
Significator

9. To encourage an individual owner to restrain animals that are obnoxious.

One of the most common sources of aggravation can be irresponsible individuals who allow their pets to run loose or otherwise be obnoxious, annoying their neighbors and often endangering the pets themselves. This can be due to either a lack of training or a lack of restraint, or in some way failing to meet the animal's needs. This spell seeks a humane way to solve such problems after talking to the owner in question or to the proper authorities has failed to get results. Rather than taking revenge on the animal (as many unhappy neighbors might be tempted to do), this spell encourages the owner to take better care of the pet, which includes enforcing the proper restraints.

The top row of cards shows the owner and the action he or she needs to take. Both the Chariot and Temperance are cards pertaining to control and wise management. The lower row of cards shows the animal in question being properly restrained, as the Eight of Swords means forced restraint.

If you wish to use accessories for this spell, white candles, flowers, gems, and cloths will suggest purity of intent. If possible set up a picture or pictures of the irresponsible owner and his or her animals; otherwise, if you can get hair, fur, feathers, etc., these will help establish a contact point for the spell.

To perform this spell, you may use the ritual provided in chapter 1, improvise a ritual of your own, or just proceed by laying out the cards and doing the following meditation, visualization, and affirmation.

Meditation and Visualization

Lay out the cards when you come to the appropriate point in the spell.

First lay down the Chariot, the animal owner's Significator and Temperance in turn. Gaze at the owner's picture, if you have one; otherwise visualize him or her clearly. Visualize him or her taking the action necessary to keep his or her pet under control (building a better fence or cage, keeping the animal indoors, etc.), while at the same time seeing that all of the animal's needs are met.

Next, lay out the animal's Significator card and the Eight of Swords. Meditate on the image in the Eight of Swords which shows a woman bound and unable to move. In conjunction with this, picture the obnoxious pet turned into a likeable animal, restrained and well behaved.

After you have finished meditating on the cards and visualizations, carefully, and with as much feeling as you can, recite the following affirmation.

Affirmation

"(Name of owner),
the owner of (name of pet),
realizes now that he/she
has allowed his/her pet
to become a nuisance and a misery
to all who must come in contact with it.
Because I have cast this spell
he/she now provides adequate restraints
and also provides better care of his/her pet.
He/she now gives love to the pet,
and the animal becomes a joy to all.
So be it!"

You may consider the spell closed at this point, or you may close the spell as desired.

Artistic and Creative Concerns

10. For help in drawing out creative abilities, gaining inspiration and fresh ideas.

*I*n this spell, the Moon represents the creative potential of the unconscious mind, and the Star stands for inspiration from inner planes. The Magician stands for the individual's ability to realize these potentials. This layout shows the process of drawing down these powers and channeling them.

If you wish to use accessories for this spell, purple or violet candles, crystals and gemstones, flowers, and cloth may be used, as these colors inspire creativity, intuition, and inspiration. If convenient, you may also lay some of the tools of your art or craft out in the ritual area.

This spell is best performed shortly before you are ready to begin work on a creative project. You may perform this spell as often as you like.

To perform this spell, you may use the ritual provided in chapter 1, improvise a ritual of your own, or just proceed by laying out the cards and doing the following meditation, visualization, and affirmation.

Meditation and Visualization

Lay out the cards when you come to the appropriate point in the ritual.

First set down the Moon. Picture yourself standing on the shore of a lake, under a moonlit sky. Imagine how refreshing it would feel to walk slowly into the water, letting it lap around your feet.

Next, set the Star in place. Envision yourself still standing in the moonlit lake while stretching your arms upward to the sky above. (At this point stretch your arms out and make a slow, wide, circular motion.) Imagine that you can feel a special power—creative energy and inspiration—dropping like tears from the stars. This energy falls onto you like a gentle rain and you imbibe its essence.

Finally, lay down the Magician. Visualize yourself drawing in this energy as it falls from the sky. Feel this power being drawn by magnetic forces through your hands, your eyes, and the rest of your body.

After you have finished meditating on the cards and visualizations, carefully, and with as much feeling as you can, recite the following affirmation.

Affirmation

"At this time and in this place
I reach forward with my mind
into time and into space!
I reach out to times that have been,
and which shall be,
and which shall never be.
I draw in power.
I draw in images.
I draw in words.
I draw in feelings.
I draw back within myself things
that have never been seen
nor heard nor felt before.
To these images I give life
so that others know the magic,
the beauty, and the mystery that I have sought
and found within myself,
and in the world around me,
and in the far stars
strewn like jewels on the velvet-black sky.
So it is and so shall it be!"

You may consider the spell closed at this point, or you may close the spell as desired.

11. For success in the arts and other areas that call on creative abilities.

*I*n this spell, a simple three-card layout is used to make a positive and concise statement. Inspiration, talent, and creativity (the Star) are channeled by the Magician, resulting in success and acclaim (the Sun). Considering that our Sun is actually a star, the individual figuratively becomes "a star."

If you wish to use accessories for this spell, candles, flowers, crystals and gemstones, and cloth can be purple or violet for inspiration and creativity, gold for shining success, or a combination of those two colors. If convenient, you may also include tools of your art or craft in the arrangement.

To perform this spell, you may use the ritual provided in chapter 1, improvise a ritual of your own, or just proceed by laying out the cards and doing the following meditation, visualization, and affirmation.

Meditation and Visualization

Lay out the cards when you come to the appropriate point in the spell.

First, lay down the Star. Visualize yourself standing on the peak of a great mountain, watching the stars which seem to be whirling about you. As you watch, you see gold and silver sparks of energy flying from the stars.

Next, set down the Magician. Imagine yourself as the Magician, reaching out your hands, and drawing to you these sparks of energy that you see. (At this point, stretch your arms and spread your fingers.) Feel the energy being drawn through your fingertips, your hands, your eyes, and all of the pores in your body.

Now, lay down the Sun. Feel the energy which you have drawn in surging through you, and creating about you a shining golden aura. The energy field about you causes you to glow like a sun—ever brighter, and ever more brilliant.

After you have finished meditating on the cards and visualizations, carefully, and with as much feeling as you can, recite the following affirmation.

Affirmation

"I draw from the magic of the cosmos,
and from the powers within me
this magic that is reflected outwards
like a golden sun!
And from this radiant magic,
I, as well as others, do benefit.
Magic, beauty, and mystery are with me
as I transmit this special magic
and others see its value,
I receive the recognition I desire.
Thus am I able
to continue to work my craft!
So it is and so shall it be!"

You may consider the spell closed at this point, or you may close the spell as desired.

Beauty, Health, and Fitness

Significator

12. For a woman: for help in working toward beauty, health, and fitness.

*B*eauty comes from within the soul, and from within the spirit. It is a thing of the mind, as much as it is of the body itself. If the mind and soul and spirit are set on beauty, its physical manifestation will follow. The following spells create a template of beauty for the mind and spirit. A special "glamour" will result, reshaping the physical appearance as well as creating a radiance, which will make the subject more beautiful to the eyes of all beholders.

In layout 12, the qualities bestowed by the Star, Strength, and the World are directed toward the Significator. Strength is used because it represents the application of willpower (in this case to dieting, exercising, and taking such other measures as needed). The Star is the charm and charisma emanating from inner beauty, and the World represents full physical and mental health as well as beauty.

If you wish to use accessories for this spell, you may use white candles, flowers, crystals and gemstones, and cloth to emphasize the purification and perfection of body that you strive for. Gold or silver artifacts could also be used for charisma and radiance. (Gold represents the radiance of the Sun, silver the Moon; which one you choose depends on which heavenly body you have a greater affinity for.) If you want your health and fitness program to emphasize the exercise part, you may use red accessories, as red stands for energy and activity. Incense, perfumes, or scented potpourris are also appropriate, as they suggest pride in physical beauty and sensuousness.

You may also want included in the arrangement of accessories images of the ideal you would like to achieve, in pictures of beautiful models or actresses, photos of yourself at a lighter weight if you are trying to lose weight gained, a simple list of goals to achieve, and so on.

Also, if possible, set up mirrors around the edges of your layout, so that they will reflect multiple images of the Tarot cards as well as the ideal images you have chosen. (Mirrors have often played a role in magic.)

The ritual for this spell can be performed at anytime. However, you may want to perform it at special times—perhaps before beginning a program of diet or exercise, or before or after your daily exercise session.

To enhance this rite and put yourself in the right frame of mind, it is a good idea to take a lustral bath first (see appendix 1). For this rite, be sure to dress yourself in clothing that you feel is especially flattering. Other accessories, such as jewelry and fragrance, will also help set the mood.

To perform this spell, you may use the ritual provided in chapter 1, improvise a ritual of your own, or just proceed by laying out the cards and doing the following meditation, visualization, and affirmation. (*Note:* In some of the old folklore, such as the legend of the Lorelei, hair brushing was a means by which a beautiful sorceress could raise power. If you prefer, you could brush your hair while making the following visualizations.)

Meditation and Visualization

Lay out the cards when you come to the appropriate point in the spell.

First, lay down the Significator card, which represents you. As you do this, make yourself aware of your body as it is now. Consider your general condition, your weight, and so on. Now, visualize your most idealized image of you—how you would look in your fantasies. Think about how you plan to change things for the better.

Next, lay down Strength, in the position indicated in the diagram. Visualize yourself drawing in energy with every breath you take, as well as drawing from your own inner power. Gently run your fingertips over your face, arms, and upper body. Feel this power stimulating and energizing every cell in your body. Consider that within you have the power to transform yourself.

Place the Star next to Strength. Feel that the power that is within you has built up, making you glow with a radiant Inner Light. Know that others will be able to see this light and will find your beauty compelling.

Finally, set down the World. Visualize yourself as you will look after you have achieved your ideal. Visualize yourself enjoying well-being, health, popularity, and success as the result. Know that even while you visualize these things, these transformations are taking place.

After you have finished meditating on the cards and visualizations, carefully, and with as much feeling as you can, recite the following affirmation.

Affirmation

"I call upon the strength within me!
I call upon the powers around me!
Beauty is in me.
Beauty is with me.
Beauty shines through me.
I commit myself
to molding and shaping myself
to achieve my ideal of beauty!
I visualize my ideal image of beauty,
and this image is a template,
that my physical form now follows.
I work hard to achieve this goal!
I enjoy full health.
I radiate charm.
I am seen by all to be beautiful.
Toward this end, I am prepared to
(here, insert whatever it is you need to do:
diet, exercise, etc.)
So it is and so shall it be!"

You may consider the spell closed at this point, or you may close the spell as suggested in the rite in chapter 1, or as desired.

As a follow-up to this spell, memorize the first five lines of the affirmation and recite them upon getting up in the morning, before exercising, and generally anytime that you feel it's important to look your best.

Significator

13. For a man: for help in working toward health, fitness, and good looks.

*I*n this layout, the qualities bestowed by the Magician, the Star, and the Sun are directed toward the Significator. The Magician represents the application of will (in this case, exercising, dieting, thinking positively, and taking other measures as are needed), and the development of potential. The Star represents that quality which we call charisma, and the Sun represents the happiness and success resulting from health and well-being.

Note: The preceding spell for women would also work for men, and the spell given here would also work for women. Although different cards may have male or female figures, they tend to more often represent principles, such as application of will in the

Magician and strength in the Strength card. If you would prefer more masculine images for this spell, you can go through your deck, find cards that project the images you'd like to identify with, and alter the spell accordingly.

If you wish to use accessories for this spell, you may use white candles, flowers, and cloth to emphasize the purity and perfection of body you are striving for. If you consider exercise the most important part of your regimen, you may instead use red props, as red stands for energy and activity. You may also choose to use gold or silver accessories, as these colors stand for charisma and radiance—gold for the Sun and silver for the Moon.

You may also want to include in the arrangement of accessories images that give an idea of the ideal you would like to achieve, such as pictures of athletes or actors, photos of yourself at a lighter weight (if you are trying to lose weight that you've gained), a simple list of goals to achieve, and so on.

Also, if possible, set up mirrors around the edges of your layout, so that they will reflect multiple images of the Tarot cards as well as the ideal images you have chosen. (Mirrors have traditionally played an important role in magic.)

The ritual for this spell may be performed at anytime. However, you may want to perform it at special times, perhaps just before beginning a new regimen of diet and exercise, or just before or after your daily exercise session.

To enhance this rite and put yourself in the right frame of mind, it is a good idea to take a lustral bath first (see appendix 1). Also, for this rite, be sure to wear clothing that you feel you look especially good in.

To perform this spell, you may use the ritual provided in chapter 1, improvise a ritual of your own, or just proceed by laying out the cards and doing the following meditation, visualization, and affirmation.

Meditation and Ritual

Lay out the cards when you come to the appropriate point in the spell.

First set down the Significator card, which represents you. Become aware of your own body as you do this, considering your general condition, weight, and so on. Now, think about how you will be able to change these things for the better.

Above and to the left of the Significator, lay down the Magician. Picture yourself drawing in energy with every breath you take, energy that will enable you to shape yourself into the ideal you. Flex your muscles, and feel the power surging through your body.

Next, lay down the Star. Feel that the energy, which you have drawn in, has built up and is causing you to glow with an inner light—a light that other people can see, finding you attractive and irresistible.

Finally, lay down the Sun. Picture yourself in your perfect body, enjoying health, well-being, popularity, and success. Know that even while you visualize these things the transformations are taking place.

After you have finished meditating on the cards and visualizations, carefully, and with as much feeling as you can, recite the following affirmation.

Affirmation

"I call upon the strength within me!
I call upon the powers around me!
I here commit myself
to molding and shaping myself
to achieve my ideal form!
I visualize my ideal physical image,
and this image is a template
that my own form now follows.
I work hard to achieve this goal
by strength of will
and by strength of arm!
I better myself day by day,
and with each day I become stronger,
better built, and more self-confident.
Toward this end I am prepared to
(insert whatever it is that you need to do:
diet, exercise, etc.)
So it is and so shall it be!"

You may consider the spell closed at this point, or you may close the spell as suggested in the rite in chapter 1, or as desired.

<table>
<tr>
<td>

Significator

</td>
<td>

</td>
<td>

</td>
</tr>
</table>

14. To project charm.

*I*n this spell, the qualities of the Star, found within the individual, are radiated outward. These qualities include charisma, charm, grace, beauty, poise, inspiration, and magic. The Magician stands for the ability to channel and radiate these qualities.

If you wish to use accessories for this spell, gold or silver candles, crystals and gemstones, metals, flowers, and cloth may be used. Both gold and silver represent radiance. Gold, which is solar, would be appropriate for a more outgoing, gregarious type of personality, whereas silver, the lunar color, would represent a more subtle charm. If possible, set mirrors up around the edge of your arrangement of cards and other accessories so that multiple images will be reflected (mirror magic will especially help build the power here). To set a mood for this spell, it will also be helpful to wear clothes, jewelry, and fragrance that are especially flattering to you and make you feel "magical."

The ritual for this spell can be performed at anytime, though you may especially want to perform it just before a special event when you will be meeting lots of people whom you would like to impress.

To perform this spell, you may use the ritual provided in chapter 1, improvise a ritual of your own, or just proceed by laying out the cards and doing the following meditation, visualization, and affirmation. *Note:* In some of the old folklore, such as the legend of the Lorelei, hair brushing was a means by which a beautiful fey or sorceress could raise power. If you're a woman with long hair, you could brush your hair while making the following visualizations.

Meditation and Visualization

When you come to the appropriate point in the spell, lay out the cards according to the diagram.

First lay down the Significator, the card which you have chosen to represent you. Visualize yourself standing amid a sea of stars. As you focus on your visualization, picture yourself looking more and more like your ideal self—sparkling and radiant.

Next, set down the Magician. Standing before your card layout, reach out your arms and make a wide, circular motion in front of you with your hands, at the same time visualizing yourself as a powerful sorcerer or sorceress. Feel a great magical energy pulsing within you, coursing through your body, and expanding outward, creating a magically magnetic field around you. Imagine that this magical energy is causing more stars to blaze in the sky around you and a garden of flowers to spring into bloom at your feet.

Finally, set the Star in position. Know that the glow of energy within you has become so expansive that it will continue to radiate and will reach out to touch and dazzle everyone you meet.

After you have finished meditating on the cards and visualizations, carefully, and with as much feeling as you can, recite the following affirmation.

Affirmation

"Magic flows through me
and beauty shines from me.
Magic and beauty
I weave around me.
Every person that I encounter
feels the compelling charm
and sees the radiant glow
that shines about me like a star.
So it is and so it shall be!"

You may consider the spell closed at this point, or you may close the spell as suggested in the rite in chapter 1, or as desired.

To help this spell along, memorize the first four lines of the affirmation, and repeat them to yourself whenever you go somewhere to meet people.

15. To enhance attractiveness, particularly sexual attractiveness.

*I*n this layout, the qualities of attractiveness and compelling charm, which the Star bestows, are alchemically transformed into sexual magnetism. It is you as the Magician who channels this magical beauty into sensuality and attractiveness to the opposite sex.

If you wish to use accessories for this spell, red candles, flowers, crystals and gemstones, and cloth will signify sexual attraction and passionate love. For this spell, use a whole row of candles or other large groupings of candles (rather than the three candles, which are recommended in the rite in chapter 1). The use of incense, perfumes, or scented potpourris is also suggested, as they enhance sensuousness. To set the right mood for this spell, it is important to wear clothing, jewelry, and fragrance that you feel especially sexy in.

To perform this spell, you may use the ritual provided in chapter 1, improvise a ritual of your own, or just proceed by laying out the cards and doing the following meditation, visualization, and affirmation.

Meditation and Visualization

When you come to the appropriate point in the spell, lay the cards out according to the diagram.

First, set down the star. Visualize yourself standing under a starlit sky. As you imagine yourself gazing at the stars, you are filled with the wonder of their beauty, and you feel that the night sky is crackling with a magically electric energy.

Next, put down the Magician. Visualize yourself as the sorcerer or sorceress, able to wield great powers. Raise your left hand (both in your visualization and in reality). Imagine your left hand drawing energy down from the stars, channeling it through your body, and shaping an aura around yourself with your right hand. Feel that the aura you have built around yourself exudes a great magnetic energy.

Finally, lay down the Lovers. As you contemplate this card, visualize ethereal forms representing the other sex circle in the shadows around you. Your magnetic aura draws them to you. Imagine yourself in some of your favorite sensual fantasies. Picture yourself as a fantastically radiant individual in settings where you are meeting fascinating members of the opposite sex who find you equally fascinating! Know that this spell will cast a special glamour over you that will make your fantasies come true.

After you have finished meditating on the cards and visualizations, carefully, and with as much feeling as you can, recite the following affirmation.

Affirmation

"The flames of these candles
do reflect the flames of the stars.
And so are the flames of passion
lit within those around me!
Those who I desire,
desire me!
Those who I find attractive
are in turn attracted by the
power and magnetism
that flow through my body.

I am irresistible!

So it is,

and so it shall continue to be!"

You may consider the spell closed at this point, or you may close the spell as suggested in the rite in chapter 1, or as desired.

16. To preserve beauty and health, and to delay aging.

*T*his is a spell for persons who have reached that certain age where one begins to be concerned about the appearance of wrinkles, thinning hair, graying, etc. This spell seeks to summon up spiritual powers as well as to send a message to the subconscious mind to mitigate the usual damage done by aging and by stress.

Ordinarily, the Wheel of Fortune represents progress and change for the better, but in this layout, it is used to represent the aging process. The Hanged Man represents stasis, and is used to cross the Wheel; it shows the march of time being thwarted. The Ace of Cups provides nourishment from spiritual and emotional sources to keep body cells and systems young and healthy. The Star also stands for nourishment from these sources, as well as for continued charm and beauty. Both the Ace of Cups and the Star also bestow the emotional and spiritual riches, which are so necessary to keeping a youthful attitude.

For this spell, have prepared a cup of water, preferably a silver goblet. If you wish to use other accessories for this spell, white might be used for candles, flowers, crystals and gemstones, and cloth, as it symbolizes pure psychic energy. Green is also a good color, as it represents healing and regeneration. Blue, which represents calm and peace, may be preferred in a situation where you feel that stress is taking a heavy toll on your youth and health. Red, which stands for energy and vitality, is also an appropriate color. The color you choose depends on which needs and qualities you want to emphasize.

It will also be helpful to have included near your Tarot spell spread a picture of yourself in your prime; that is, with the looks you want to preserve. If possible, set a mirror or mirrors up around the edge of your arrangement, so the images will be reflected in the mirrors.

This is a spell that should be performed periodically, especially during the waxing Moon.

To perform this spell, you may use the ritual provided in chapter 1, improvise a ritual of your own, or just proceed by laying out the cards and doing the following meditation, visualization, and affirmation.

Meditation and Visualization

Lay out the cards when you come to the appropriate point in the spell.

First, lay down the Ace of Cups. Visualize yourself standing alongside a calm lake on a warm summer evening. Imagine that you hold your hands out, and suddenly a silver cup appears in your hands. You bend down, and dip the cup into the cool blue water. At this point, take up the cup of water that you have prepared and drink from it. Continue your visualization while you drink, imagining that as you sip slowly from the cup, savoring the fresh taste of the water, you feel a wonderful tingling sensation all over your body. The water makes you feel totally refreshed and relaxed. You are struck by the realization that you are partaking of a magical drink that will preserve you in a state of youth and beauty. You realize that you are drinking from the fountain of youth.

Next, lay down the Wheel of Fortune (on its side, as indicated in the diagram), picturing time as a great wheel, which cycles the years and seasons. Immediately lay down the Hanged Man so that it crosses the Wheel. Study the calm and contemplative look on the hanged man's youthful face. Consider how the Hanged Man represents suspension and stasis, as well as calm and reflection. As you look at this card, notice that your facial muscles and other muscles are becoming totally smoothed, totally relaxed. Know that the water you drank from the cup has given you a spiritual tranquility, which will immunize you against the stresses that bring about aging.

Finally, set down the Star. Again, visualize yourself by the lake under the evening sky. Look up to the stars, and realize that you have a special kinship with them. Realize that their power is yours to draw upon, for the very atoms that comprise your body have come across the vast distances from the stars. Stretch your arms out and visualize the stars whirling around you, until you feel your own spirit joining in the dance of the stars. Know that the magical energy that you have drawn from this spell will continue to nourish you, and that you can always replenish yourself by repeating this visualization.

After you have finished meditating on the cards and visualizations, carefully, and with as much feeling as you can, recite the following affirmation.

Affirmation

"I have tasted the waters of life!

My spirit soars,

and my body is regenerated.

I am nourished by powers from within

and powers from without.

Every cell and every system in my body

is nourished and refreshed.

My mind is tranquil

and I am filled with peace.

The vast river of the cosmos

flows past me.

Time stands still for me.

The years wheel by,

yet they have no power over me

for the stars are my kindred,

and their power sustains me.

So it is, and so it shall continue to be!"

You may consider the spell closed at this point, or you may close the spell as suggested in the rite in chapter 1, or as desired.

The Hermit — Judgement 20 20 — 21 The World 21

17. To help reverse the aging process and recapture lost beauty.

*T*his is a spell useful for mature persons who want to repair some of the damage that aging does to the body's cells and systems. This spell should be used to complement exercise, diet, and other health-recovery programs.

In this spell, great elemental powers as well as the powers that are found within each person are invoked to transform the individual. In this concise layout, we see the infirmities of old age being replaced by vigor, health, and beauty. Here, the Hermit card is used for its graphic depiction of old age, Judgement encompasses major transformations as well as regeneration, and the World shows the individual in his or her most ideal state of being.

If you wish to use accessories for this spell, the colors red and orange, which stand for energy and vitality, may be used for candles, crystals and gemstones, flowers, and cloth to lay the cards upon. Or, if preferred, the color green may be used, as green represents healing and regeneration. White, which represents pure psychic energy, is also appropriate. Your choice of color depends upon which qualities you prefer to emphasize.

It will also be helpful to have as an accessory in your arrangement a picture of yourself taken at a time when you were younger and enjoyed full health. If possible, set up a mirror or mirrors around the edge of your arrangement so that all of the images will be reflected.

The ritual for this spell can be performed at anytime, although it would be helpful to perform it when the Moon goes into its waxing phase, right after a new (dark) Moon.

To perform the spell, you may use the ritual provided in chapter 1, improvise a ritual of your own, or just proceed by laying out the cards and doing the following meditation, visualization, and affirmation.

Meditation and Visualization

When you come to the appropriate point in the spell, lay out the cards as indicated in the diagram.

First, lay down the Hermit. Visualize yourself walking alongside the sea in a mountainous coastal region. As you walk along, consider how the years have brought you many good things, including experience and insight. You know, however, that age and stress have also done some damage to your body, which you now intend to set about correcting. In your continuing visualization, imagine that you now see a beautiful temple, which lies before you. Visualize yourself approaching the temple, and going inside it. You walk over to and step up on a raised platform inside the temple.

Next, lay down the Judgement card. Continue your visualization: you are standing on the platform in the temple. Suddenly, you realize that you know the secret of the temple, a place of great power where you can call light and power into your own body. Stretch out your arms and feel energy flowing into you from the walls of the temple, from the mountains, from the sea, from the stars in the sky. Feel your fingertips tingle with an electric force as vitality enters through your fingers and spreads throughout your body. By now the force has become so strong that your body is bathed in a light that has never been seen before, casting a glow on the temple, mountains, and water around you.

Finally, lay down the World. In your continued visualization, lower your arms slowly, and take in a deep breath of relaxation. You realize that the glow is now beginning to fade, but you know what has happened: the energy you summoned has revitalized every cell and system in your body. You look down at your hands. Yes, you have changed; you are younger. You can see that your hands are already beginning to look smoother, firmer, and more elastic. You walk away from the temple jauntily, happily; the mission has been successful. (Know that you can come back here again when you feel you need more revitalization. Just take a few moments of relaxation when needed, and visualize yourself exploring or just relaxing in the temple.)

After you have finished meditating on the cards and visualizations, carefully, and with as much feeling as you can, recite the following affirmation.

Affirmation

"I call upon the power that flows within me!

I draw power from the elements around me!

I call strength from the rocks, magic from the stars,

energy from the seas.

Power that grows!

Power that flows!

Power that transmutes me!

As I do breathe this power in and out,

every cell in my body shall be renewed.

I feel the tingling of power now,

as every cell and every bodily system

is restored and refreshed!

And with every breath I take,

I become more energetic.

I become younger,

I become more beautiful!

So it is, and so it shall continue to be!"

You may consider the spell closed at this point, or you may close the spell as suggested in the rite in chapter 1, or as desired.

Business

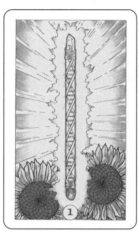

18. For success in starting a new business.

*T*his is a spell that one would perform before starting out on a major business venture. It calls upon that vast source of psychic energy that can be found within all of us, and directs this energy to get the new business off to a strong and auspicious start.

In this concise layout, the Magician stands for the individual directing his or her talents, resources, and energies into the new business venture, which is represented by the Ace of Wands. The Sun is the result: success, growth, and prosperity.

If you wish to use accessories for this spell, use green candles, flowers, crystals and gemstones, and cloth to lay the cards upon, to symbolize growth, and/or use gold accessories to symbolize prosperity. If possible, include near your card arrangement any items that will symbolize your endeavor, such as tools of your trade, pictures of the place where you will be doing business, and so on. You may also have your business suit hanging nearby, neatly pressed and ready to go.

This spell may be performed at anytime, but it is most likely that you would choose to perform it before making a major move in starting up your new business: upon first making your decision, before you apply for permits or loans, upon renting an office or getting a key piece of equipment, etc.

To perform this spell, you may use the ritual provided in chapter 1, improvise a ritual of your own, or just proceed by laying out the cards and doing the following meditation, visualization, and affirmation.

Meditation and Visualization

When ready, lay the cards out according to the diagram.

First, put the Magician in place. Visualize yourself as a master magician or sorceress, savvy and powerful. You know within the depths of your heart that you have the power to make things happen. In your visualization, imagine yourself raising a magic wand high above you, and pulling power from the vast cosmos into your wand, causing your wand to glow with the energy.

Next, set down the Ace of Wands. Continue to visualize the wand, watching as it actually pulses with the energy flowing through it. Now visualize yourself waving your wand before you. The wand makes a crackling sound and sparks fly out, sparks which materialize into images of your plans. These images show you starting out, working hard at your line of business, what sort of work you will do, where you will be located, the money you're going to make, what you're going to do with the money, and so on.

Finally, add the Sun to the layout. Think of the word "success," and the warm feeling and glowing image this word suggests. Again, visualize your new business getting off to a good start and growing strong, just like a seed that germinates and matures into a flower that reaches toward the Sun.

After you have finished meditating on the cards and visualizations, carefully, and with as much feeling as you can, recite the following affirmation.

Affirmation

"With this spell
I call forth power!
I call upon the power within me
for within me is the power
to make my plans a reality.
Energy and power
I direct to this, my new venture.
All is in readiness as I now prepare myself
to actualize my dreams,
my plans, my ideals.
I persevere against all hardships
and carry through.
I am busy, and I enjoy being busy!
I work hard and I make it!
I achieve success and prosperity
From this time forth, so it shall be!"

You may consider the spell closed at this point, or you may close the spell as suggested in the rite in chapter 1, or as desired.

✳

19. For general business success.

*T*his is a spell intended to give a magical boost to an already established business. Whereas the previous spell summoned the energy needed to direct into a new business venture, this spell emphasizes financial increase: encouraging growth, bringing in more customers, and increasing prosperity.

The Three of Wands is the focal card in this pyramidal layout. It is the card that best stands for "business" per se and it shows that business is brisk. It is bolstered by the Sun to assure that all is well, all elements growing and thriving, and the Ace of Pentacles for a constant flow of capital.

If you wish to use accessories for this spell, use green and/or gold candles, flowers, crystals and gemstones, and cloth. Green symbolizes growth and gold symbolizes prosperity. Have some crisp new currency or shiny new coins (or real gold or silver coins, if you have them) on hand to use in the spell. If possible, enhance your arrangement by surrounding your cards with tools of your trade or other items that are important to your business, pictures of yourself at work, pictures of your place of business, and so on. You may also have your favorite business suit hanging nearby, so that some of the magical energy raised will cling to it.

This spell may be used at anytime, although spells for increase and growth are traditionally performed during the waxing Moon. Because of some of the imagery that follows, I recommend doing this spell on a sunny morning during the Moon's waxing phase.

To perform this spell, you may use the ritual provided in chapter 1, improvise a ritual of your own, or just proceed by laying out the cards and doing the following meditation, visualization, and affirmation.

Meditation and Visualization

When ready, lay out the cards according to the diagram.

First, set out the Three of Wands. Think of your own business and consider how you have within you the power to meet all the challenges to make your business expand and prosper. Visualize yourself as the master or mistress of all you survey, a person who does very well for yourself, and for those whom you love.

To the left of this, put down the Ace of Pentacles. Visualize yourself receiving money in one of your regular business transactions. Now, take up your coins or currency and rub these between your fingers. As you do so, visualize your business increasing steadily, as you take in more and more money. Picture yourself as having the Midas touch: where you go an avalanche of pure gold follows and you feel great about it! For you, it comes as easily as can be.

At last, lay the Sun down to the right of the Three of Wands. Feel the warmth of the Sun beating down on you (if it is not possible for you to do this standing in sunlight, just imagine yourself standing under a bright, sunlit sky with the Sun's rays upon you). The Sun makes you feel that you are bathed in gold. You reach your fingers up, and imagine how everything you touch will take on a golden glow. At this point, take up the tools of your trade or other articles associated with your business. Envision these items becoming warmer and glowing with the power that a mere touch from you has transferred to them. Now, envision your own image of success: perhaps an image of yourself dressed for business, walking out of your building, walking out to a large and handsome car that is waiting for you. You pause by your sleek, new vehicle and look back at the building that is yours, feeling a warm glow of satisfaction.

After you have finished meditating on the cards and visualizations, carefully, and with as much feeling as you can, recite the follow affirmation.

Affirmation

"Success is mine!
I draw strength, and I draw power.
I am the one who makes it happen,
my field of endeavor,
the business that I have chosen to do,
grows and thrives.
Money comes in,
money flows through my hands
in ever greater amounts;
better than it has in the past.
The forces are behind me.
I'm on a roll,
and I'm in control of it.
I am riding a wave of golden sunlight.
This it is, this it shall be
from this time forth!"

You may consider the spell closed at this point, or you may close the spell as suggested in the rite in chapter 1, or as desired.

20. For success in starting a home business.

*T*his spell is for those who seek the convenience and other benefits of running a business out of the home.

With its four cards, this layout suggests the four corners and foundations of a house. The number four traditionally stands for stability, material comfort, and security—things that are generally of importance to those interested in starting a home business.

All of the ingredients are here: the Four of Wands can refer to both a home and a place of business. The Ace of Wands typically represents the starting up of a business or enterprise, and the Three of Wands denotes that the business will be active and thriving. The Nine of Pentacles represents self-sufficiency, and, in some cases, self-employment (as well as a promise of prosperity and security).

If you wish to use accessories for this spell, green for candles, crystals and gemstones, floral arrangements, and cloths is suggested.

Green represents growth as well as financial security and prosperity. Place a slip of paper with the name and description of your planned business above the card layout. If possible, have special tools of your trade and other items important to your planned business in your arrangement.

This spell may be best performed in the area of your home where you intend to work at your business. Although this spell can be performed at anytime, you may wish to do it upon making a major move in starting up your home business, upon first making your decision before you apply for permits or loans, upon getting a key piece of equipment, etc.

To perform this spell, you may use the ritual provided in chapter 1, improvise a ritual of your own, or just proceed by laying out the cards and doing the following meditation, visualization, and affirmation.

Meditation and Visualization

When ready, lay the cards out according to the diagram.

Set down the Four of Wands first. As you do so, visualize your home office or work area set up and ready to go. Consider the benefits of being able to work in the comfort and convenience of your own home—a home fully appointed for all your business needs.

Next, place the Ace of Wands above the Four of Wands. Think of how you'll pour all your energy into your new home business. Visualize yourself in your comfortable home setting, working hard, and enjoying what you're doing. Take up any tools of your trade or other items important to your business, which you may have near the arrangement. Handle them while you think of yourself working hard as well as enthusiastically at your new business.

Set the Three of Wands down next, as you try to imagine a typical working day in your own business. Picture the little details of a busy and thriving enterprise: lots of things to do, lots of customers, all the business you need and want.

Lay the Nine of Pentacles down last, envisioning the ultimate sense of security and satisfaction you hope to attain with your home business. Visualize yourself doing the work and other things you enjoy, and maintaining yourself in the style you want.

After you have finished meditating on the cards and visualizations, carefully, and with as much feeling as you can, recite the following affirmation.

Affirmation

"With this spell,

I bring power to my resolve.

I start my own business.

I enjoy the advantages and benefits

of making my home my place of business.

As I start this business

not only do I cast a spell,

but I also work unceasingly

to make my business a success.

I have chosen a work I enjoy,

and business will be good.

As I cast this spell,

I cast forth my will!

I charge this spell

to make word of my product spread.

Let those who can use my product

be attracted to me

and see what I have to offer.

In this way,

the ends I desire shall be achieved:

comfort, security, and contentment.

So be it!"

You may consider the spell closed at this point, or you may close the spell as suggested in the rite in chapter 1, or as desired.

✳ ✳

21. For a general change in one's circumstances in life.

*F*or spells designed to bring about changes in one's self, one's circumstances in life, or one's environment, the important cards are the Magician, which represents the individual taking the initiative in bringing about changes, and the Wheel, which when surrounded by positive cards represents change, evolution, and progress.

This spell is designed for persons who find themselves locked into a dissatisfying and frustrating situation. This spell summons physical and psychical energies to set a chain of events in motion to bring about a new set of personal circumstances.

A step-like card arrangement is used to show improvement and advancement toward a goal. The Magician acts as a Significator card and shows the subject working hard to bring about changes (always an essential ingredient when changes are required). The Magician also invokes power from above in order to get the strength and resolve to make these changes happen. The Eight of Wands stands for movement toward goals or desires. The Wheel here represents the development of the entire set of life's circumstances and the factors, which influence their evolution.

If you wish to use accessories for this spell, the color orange may be used for candles, flowers, crystals and gemstones, and cloths, and so on, as orange stands for action directed by intellect. Red may be used instead if you wish to emphasize the vital force needed to push changes; white may be used to symbolize purity of intention and pure psychic energy.

Also, before you perform this spell, make a list of the number of ways events, actions, and/or attitudes could progress to help your circumstances change for the better. Place this list near your card arrangement.

This spell may be performed at anytime. However, times such as first thing in the morning, first day of the week, and/or first day of the month would all be auspicious times to work this magic. It would also be well to perform this rite during the Moon's waxing phase.

To perform this spell, you may use the ritual provided in chapter 1, improvise a ritual of your own, or just proceed by laying out the cards and doing the following meditation, visualization, and affirmation.

Meditation and Visualization

When ready, lay the cards out according to the diagram.

First, set the Magician in place. Envision yourself as a mighty magician or a powerful sorceress. You are intensely aware that *you* have the power to make things *happen!* Imagine that you are holding a magical wand in your right hand. In your visualization as well as in reality, stretch your left arm high over your head and feel that you are drawing in power from the cosmos around you. Feel that this energy is being pulled in through your fingertips. It flows through your body and out into the wand you are visualizing.

Next, set the Eight of Wands in place. Think of your life as it is now, then consider the changes that will make your life more ideal: a better job, better situation, and better circumstances. Think of how urgently you want to make these changes happen. Visualize yourself waving your magic wand before you, causing a shower of sparks to fly from it. The sparkling energy flows outward, and before your eyes, you see it shaping images of your near future, bringing about the changes that you need. You are surprised at how rapidly you see these changes taking place.

Finally, set down the Wheel of Fortune. Continue to visualize new things coming into your life. Imagine the happy future that will unfold as you make these things happen.

After you have finished meditating on the cards and visualizations, carefully, and with as much feeling as you can, recite the following affirmation.

Affirmation

"The time has come for a change.
The time has come to move on to something newer,
something better.
That which was done in the past
shall be prelude to an ever-greater future,
moving onward and upward.
Changes are coming
with one action leading rapidly to another.

The forces are set in motion.
Inexorably I move
toward the goals that I desire.
A new stage of evolution is before me!
The power I summon
turns the wheel of heaven.
The changes begin with this spell
and continue as I better myself
and all that is around me.
So it is and so it shall continue to be!"

You may consider the spell closed at this point, or you may close the spell as suggested in the rite in chapter 1, or as desired.

22. To get away from a bad environmental situation.

*T*his spell is essentially a variation on the previous spell. It differs in that it is more specific about the type of change desired. This spell is for the individual who is unhappy with the environment in which he or she is forced to live and wants to be physically removed to another place. "Environment" can refer to the home, the workplace, a geographical area, and so on.

This layout also takes the form of stairs. In this case, the steps are shown to lead up to happier surroundings.

The Wheel of Fortune denotes a fortuitous set of events and circumstances that cause changes to take place and promise ongoing progress. The Eight of Cups traditionally represents leaving one way of life behind and moving on to another one. If you want to reinforce this desire, you may place your own Significator card under the Eight of Cups (refer to the section on "Significators" in appendix 1). The World has two interpretations that are both meaningful here: it represents fulfillment, as well as happy and peaceful surroundings.

If you wish to use accessories for this spell, orange candles, flowers, crystals and gemstones, and cloth may be used, as orange stands for action directed by intellect. As an alternative, red accessories may be used to emphasize the use of vital force in affecting changes, or white may be used to signify purity of intent and pure psychic energy. If there are pictures available which suggest the type of environment you would like to be in (for example, pictures showing a comfortable home, appealing workplace, or specific geographic area), then have these pictures spread out around your ritual area.

Since this spell is intended to help you move to better surroundings, it is important to create the right mood by making the area where this spell will be performed as cheerful as possible. Somewhat in advance of working this spell, do some simple cleanup and fix up so that you will have a pleasant area in which to perform the rite. Make sure the area is well aired and decorate it with fresh flowers. Also, take special care to take a lustral bath (refer to appendix 1), and wear clean clothes that you feel comfortable and confident in.

Meditation and Visualization

This spell may be performed at anytime. However, times such as first thing in the morning, first day of the week, and/or first day of the month would all be good times to work this spell. It is also auspicious to perform such a spell during the Moon's waxing phase.

To perform the spell, you may use the ritual provided in chapter 1, improvise a ritual of your own, or just proceed by laying out the cards and doing the following meditation, visualization, and affirmation.

When ready, lay the cards out according to the diagram.

Set down the Wheel of Fortune. Think about the present environment which you are so unhappy with, then visualize the type of environment you would like to be in. Study the image of the wheel on the card and consider how life progresses in cycles. Know that a turning point will come, and your life will move into a new cycle in a new place. Many forces are at work for you.

Next, lay down the Eight of Cups. Consider how there are certain things you have learned and certain things you have achieved in your present situation—but now it is time to move on. Know that an opportunity will soon present itself and when it does, you will have everything you need (emotionally and physically) to leave your old surroundings behind and move on to a better place.

Finally, set the World card in place. Strongly visualize yourself in the sort of place where you would like to be, with all of its good points, all of its challenges, all of its beauty. If you have pictures that suggest the type of environment that you would like to be in, take them up at this time. Look them over and handle them while you continue this meditation. Sense the satisfaction and well being that will be yours—a sense of happiness that will make you feel like dancing.

After you have finished meditating on the cards and visualizations, carefully, and with as much feeling as you can, recite the following affirmation.

Affirmation

"With this spell and with these cards
the forces of change are set in motion.
My life enters a new cycle
as surely as the wheel of fate does turn.
I leave behind all that is old and outworn,
all that gives pain, all that gives stress,
and move to a new life and a new situation.
I create new surroundings
where I am much happier,
much more able to enjoy life.
In working toward this goal,
I do not cease from striving.
I am alert to every opportunity that comes my way,
while I make every opportunity to transform
and brighten all that is around me.
This do I vow!
So it is and so shall it be!"

You may consider the spell closed at this point, or you may close the spell as suggested in the rite in chapter 1, or as desired.

✳

Significator

23. To encourage positive changes within a person, institution, or organization.

*T*his is a spell that could be applied to a broad range of situations. The tendency for individuals, institutions, and organizations to resist changes for the better is a frustration that all of us encounter all too often. If you are currently running up against stubborn resistance to progress and improvement, this spell will help nudge those involved to make needed changes.

This spell uses a step-like layout to suggest upward movement and progress. It shows the subject of the spell undergoing the processes needed to bring about advancement and reform.

The Significator represents the individual, institution, or organization in question. To choose an appropriate Significator, refer to the section on "Significators," appendix 1. The Wheel of Fortune represents all of the factors and forces that are to be invoked to stimulate change. Judgement represents major changes and improvements.

If you wish to use accessories for this spell, try to obtain something that belongs to the subject in order to help establish a magical link. If the subject is an impersonal institution, try to obtain something like the company's letterhead or its annual report. Place whatever items you have obtained near your card layout. For accessories such as candles, crystals and gemstones, flowers, and cloth to lay the cards upon, red, orange, and/or white would be appropriate colors to choose from. Red could represent the energy and impulse needed to set changes in motion. Orange also represents directed energy. White stands for psychic energy as well as purity of intention.

This spell can be performed at anytime, although the Moon's waxing phase is especially auspicious.

To perform this spell, you may use the ritual provided in chapter 1, improvise a ritual of your own, or just proceed by laying out the cards and doing the following meditation, visualization, and affirmation.

Meditation and Visualization

When ready, lay the cards out according to the diagram.

First, set down the card that you consider to be the best Significator for the person or organization to be influenced by this spell. If you were able to obtain anything belonging to the subject, pick it up, feel it, and stroke it. In your mind's eye, picture the individual or institution in question. Think about the problems you have encountered with the subject, and how positive changes are needed in order to make life easier for everyone concerned.

Next, set down The Wheel of Fortune. Picture the steps that need to be taken for this person or organization to gain the consciousness and the desire to make improvements. Picture these steps being taken in a realistic manner: things being discussed, considered, action being taken, how it would be taken, who would manage it, how it would be accomplished, and how it would continue to be carried out in the future.

Finally, set the Judgement card in place. Visualize the subject entity as being transformed quickly and permanently into something new and better.

After you have finished meditating on the cards and visualizations, carefully, and with as much feeling as you can, recite the following affirmation.

Affirmation

"With this spell and with these cards
I set in motion the forces of change!
I call for improvements
and alterations of attitude
in (name of subject).
The forces of circumstance,
and chance, and serendipity
work toward this change!
This change comes magically from within.
This spell lives and grows,
grows and continues,
continues and expands.
The results are good,
and get ever better as time progresses.
(Subject) has a new outlook,
(subject) takes more positive actions.
(Subject) gives better treatment to all concerned.
These transformations are made
and shall continue.
So it is and so shall it be!"

You may consider the spell closed at this point, or you may close the spell as suggested in the rite in chapter 1, or as desired.

24. For help in adjusting to a difficult or traumatic change of circumstances.

*T*his spell is designed to help ease the process of transition for a person who must make a difficult readjustment. It seeks to enable the subject to face the inevitable changes as well as to maintain or regain control of his or her life and make the best out of the situation at hand.

This layout suggests a downward staircase, which gently leads the individual into a new phase of life, where he or she will have the power to make his or her own happiness.

The Wheel of Fortune depicts the cycles of the individual's life as well as the circumstances that have brought him or her to this point. The Magician shows the individual adapting to change and mastering the new situation. The World stands for the new life that the subject will build—a life that is fulfilling and optimistic.

Accessories for this spell may include candles, flowers, crystals and gemstones, and cloth. Green would be a suitable color to use for accessories if you want to emphasize healing, resilience, adaptation, and readjustment. If you feel that extra energy is what is needed to make the readjustment, then use red or orange accessories. Brown, which represents "rootedness," is a color that could be used where the trauma is the result of being uprooted or insecure.

To perform this spell, you may use the ritual provided in chapter 1, improvise a ritual of your own, or just proceed by laying out the cards and doing the following meditation, visualization, and affirmation.

Meditation and Visualization

When ready, lay the cards out according to the diagram.

First, set down the Wheel of Fortune. Think about the changes you have undergone, and the chain of circumstances that have brought you to the present situation. (If you are doing this spell for someone else, consider as much as you know of that person's situation and what sort of events have led up to it.) Realize that things change and change is often necessary. It is the nature of the universe, and one must change with it to grow ever greater. Undergoing hardships will make you a stronger person, for the finest steel is tempered by the hottest flame.

Next, set the Magician in place. Visualize yourself as a powerful magician or sorceress. Feel a reservoir of great strength rising from within; know each person is a magician with the power to reshape circumstances. Visualize yourself as the magician standing on a barren desert. Then, imagine using your magic wand to draw power from the universe as well as power from within. Wave your wand in front of you and see the channeled power causing flowers to spring up everywhere, turning the desert into a garden.

Finally, take up the World card. Before you set it in place, hold it up and present it to each of the four directions—east, south, west, and north. Now lay the World in place. Visualize yourself in a setting, that has been beautified and improved through your own effort. Visualize yourself in a situation where you have created your own happiness and found fulfillment in spite of outward circumstances, hardships, and difficult readjustments.

After you have finished meditating on the cards and visualizations, carefully, and with as much feeling as you can, recite the following affirmation.

Affirmation

"With these cards and with this spell,

I summon powers of resilience and renewal.

I summon powers from within,

and powers from without.

I summon the power to help me face the world as it is,

and as it must of necessity be in the future.

I summon the power to help me make my own happiness.

I meet this new and challenging situation with confidence.

There is peace.

There is healing.

There is new understanding.

This do I will! So will it be!"

You may consider the spell closed at this point, or you may close the spell as suggested in the rite in chapter 1, or as desired.

Children

25. For success in starting a family.

*T*his is a spell that would be of interest to a couple who has decided they are now ready for the big step of starting a family. This spell will make their first efforts in making a family more auspicious. It could also be of some help to persons who have been trying to start a family, but have not so far been successful. (For this spell, it is presumed that you already have a stable relationship and a secure home.)

In this sample layout, the Ace of Wands shows energy directed toward the start of something promising—in this case a family. The Ten of Cups is the focal card, showing an ideal family situation. The Sun is included because it represents children as well as success and happiness.

For the purpose of this spell, obtain one small baby item to be included near your Tarot card layout. Anything that can be handled during the meditation will do: a rattle or other colorful baby toy, a layette item, a bib or baby bottle, a family heirloom baby item, etc. The item chosen should be something that makes you feel good by just looking at it. Since this is also something that you will want to present to your first-born child, you should make sure that there is nothing in its contents or construction that could harm a baby. This is a generalized spell, so it's probably best to use something that's not sex-specific. (For a sex-specific spell, refer to spells 27 and 28 on conceiving a baby girl or a baby boy.)

If you wish to use other accessories for this spell, red candles, flowers, crystals and gemstones, and cloth to lay the cards upon can be used; traditionally this color is associated with conception. Red can also stand for the energy and vitality that you are ready to invest in building a family.

This is a spell to perform once both partners have firmly decided that they are ready to commit themselves to having a family. The hopeful mother-to-be should choose the best date to perform this spell by calculating the best time for conception. You may also want to take into consideration various seasonal and astrological factors. This spell should be performed in the evening. For best results, both partners should participate.

To perform this spell, use the ritual provided in chapter 1, improvise a ritual of your own, or just proceed by laying out the cards and doing the visualization and affirmation.

Meditation and Visualization

When ready, set the Ace of Wands in place in the position indicated on the diagram. Then both of you should hold hands while you think about your mutual decision to have a family. Meditate on your desire to have children and on all of the energy and effort you are willing to put into this. Visualize the action that you will take to bring this about. Visualize as best you can the sequence of events that you hope to set in motion: the stages of pregnancy, childbirth, a baby growing into a toddler and on into the other stages of childhood, the birth of additional children, if you want them, and so on. After a few moments, both of you should put your right hand on the small baby item that you have provided for this spell. Both should repeat, "This small item is a token of the commitment that we are ready to make."

Next, set the Ten of Cups in place. Visualize the type of family life that you plan to create. Visualize yourselves as happy parents with all the children you want, living in the warm and comfortable environment you will provide.

Last, lay down the Sun. Picture your family life as you hope it will be several years from now. Visualize the group of you together, standing in the warm light of the Sun, enjoying the happiness, love, devotion, and sense of togetherness that you have achieved. After you have finished meditating on the cards and visualizations, carefully, and with as much feeling as you can, recite the following affirmation.

Affirmation

"With these cards and with this spell
we call upon all good and helpful powers!
Hear us and aid us now for we desire to start a family!
We bring energy to start our family!
We bring love to start our family!
We bring commitment to start our family!
This small item (hold up the baby item)
is a token of the commitment
that we are ready to make.
We are ready to love our children,

we are ready to enjoy our children,

and we are ready to have as many children as we want.

So it is, and so it shall be!"

Seal this spell with hugs and kisses, followed by the action necessary to start your family. You may consider the spell closed at this point, or you may close the spell as suggested in the rite in chapter 1 or as desired.

Significator

26. For strength, health, safety, and ease of childbirth.

*T*his spell calls upon the qualities, which will carry a woman through the difficulties of pregnancy and childbirth. The power of this spell is at its strongest when the parents-to-be perform it together, so the directions are written to be followed by an expectant couple. However, if this spell is performed alone by an expectant mother or is performed on behalf of another person, you should alter the directions as necessary.

In this layout, the Significator card representing the mother-to-be is flanked by Strength, which bestows all the qualities this card implies, plus the Sun, which stands for children, as well as for happiness and success. The Empress crowns this pyramidal layout. The Empress stands for motherhood and fertility, and promises that all will be well.

For this spell, you may obtain something that can be used as a special charm, and which will be kept near the card arrangement, to be charged with power during the spell. This charm can then be kept near the expectant mother throughout her pregnancy. (This charm is optional and is to be thought of as a nice little "extra"; do not feel that you have to be dependent on it. Your luck will not be affected if you lose the charm or do not always have it near you.) A small baby item, such as a rattle, can be used as a charm for this spell. The charm can also take the form of jewelry, a statuette, or a picture. Such a charm may depict some traditional maternity symbol. (Figures of pregnant women believed to have been used as charms date back to prehistoric times.) Animals such as the rabbit, which is famous for its pregnancies, or the cat, which is known as a devoted mother, also figure as good luck charms. These animals are also sacred to a number of ancient mother goddesses. The hippopotamus was used by the Egyptians to symbolize the goddess Tau-urt, who was the patroness of pregnancy; so if you can obtain a hippopotamus figure (and also have a sense of humor to go with it), this would also be an appropriate charm. If you are able to obtain emblems or figurines through a history museum gift shop or art catalog, you may also acquire other ancient goddesses who were reputed to help in childbirth, including Isis, Meskhent, Demeter, Diana, Juno Lucina, Freya, Parvati, and Kuan-yin. Traditional Madonna symbols would also be good for this purpose.

If you wish to use other accessories for this spell, red candles, flowers, crystals and gemstones, and cloth to lay the cards upon can be used, because this color has traditionally been associated with conception, childbirth, and motherhood. Red can also stand for the energy and vitality required to carry the mother-to-be through pregnancy and childbirth. White is also a good color to use, as it stands for purity, spiritual strength, and energy. If you are performing this spell on behalf of someone who is not present, have near the card layout a picture or some other personal belonging of hers.

To perform this spell, use the ritual provided in chapter 1, improvise a ritual of your own, or just proceed by laying out the cards and doing the meditation, visualization, and affirmation.

Meditation and Visualization

When ready, set the expectant mother's Significator card in place. Then you (the expectant couple) should hold hands while considering your happiness upon learning about the pregnancy. Now, look at the Significator card and consider the many changes the expectant mother is now undergoing and will continue to undergo.

Next, lay Strength down to the left of the Significator. Visualize the expectant mother in a state of perfect health. Visualize her having the energy and strength needed to carry the strain that pregnancy places on the body and the mind.

Now, place the Empress above the Significator as shown in the diagram. Visualize the expectant mother going through all of the stages of pregnancy. Visualize as ideal a pregnancy as you can imagine, calling upon any sentimental images you may have of the "Earth Mother" personality and experience. Visualize the mother having an idyllic pregnancy, culminating with giving birth safely and easily in an ideal setting.

Finally, set the Sun in place. Visualize a beautiful baby in a state of hearty health and happiness. Both mother and father should now put their hands on the mother's stomach and try to sense a bond with the presence within.

At this point, the father-to-be should use both hands to draw a protective egg or aura around his wife. To do this, he should visualize cosmic power coursing through his body, then will a surge of psychic power to flow out from his hands. He then holds his hands over her head and works his way downward, moving his hands in small circular motions or such other motions he feels comfortable with, using the energy to shape a protective force field. Seal this action with a kiss.

Note: If this spell is being performed on behalf of a person not present, lay her picture or personal belonging over the Significator card and make the hand motions over the card layout. Take similar actions for the consecration of the charm, which follows. If you are performing this spell alone, modify the instructions and shape the force field with your own hands.

Next, take up the item which you have chosen to use as a charm, then both of you press the charm to the mother's abdomen while saying together the following affirmation.

Affirmation

"We call upon all good and helpful powers!

Hear us and aid us now

through pregnancy and childbirth.

We ask for protection.

We ask for strength.

We ask for full health.

(Name of mother) is surrounded by your protective power.

This small item (referring to the charm)

shall also hold protective power.

It shall be kept near (mother)

to give extra strength and protection.

So it is, and so shall it be!"

Place the charm back by the card layout for the time being, and seal the spell with another kiss. You may consider the spell closed at this point, or you may close the spell as suggested in the rite in chapter 1, or as desired.

27. To encourage the conception of a baby girl.

*M*editation on the female symbolism in this layout emphasizes that a child of the female sex is desired.

This spell ought to be used in conjunction with various popular techniques for influencing the sex of children at conception. We can't go into these techniques here (they concern the balance of chemicals in the womb as well as the timing of conception). Ask your doctor about these techniques, or research them in medical books.

Note: I tend to be leery about trying to influence the sex of unborn children, since I feel that there may be karmic reasons for certain persons to be born to certain parents, and that a child's soul should choose the sex with which it can best express itself.

However, I realize that having children of a certain sex can he very important to some parents, and have designed this spell in recognition of this need.

The power of this spell is at its strongest when the parents-to-be perform it together, so the directions are written to be followed by an expectant couple. However, if this spell is performed alone by an expectant mother or is performed on behalf of another person, you should alter the directions accordingly.

In this spell, the Empress represents fertility and conception. The World is the focal card, here used to represent a girl resulting from the conception. (Of course the World generally isn't restricted to representing females and female concerns. However, as there are no cards specifically designed to represent baby boys or baby girls, you can use cards that have pictures that suggest that which you desire.) The Star can also be used to represent a female child, in addition to its regular meanings of good luck, creativity, and fertility.

As an accessory for this spell, obtain one small baby girl's item to act as a charm and to be included near your Tarot card layout. Anything that can he handled during the meditation will do: a pink rattle or other feminine baby toy, a layette item, a family heirloom baby item, etc. The item chosen should be something that makes you feel good by just looking at it. Since this is also something that you will want to present to your newborn child, you should make sure that there is nothing in its contents or construction that could harm a baby

If you wish to use other accessories for this spell, pink candles, flowers, crystals and gemstones, and cloth to lay the cards upon can be used, as in our society this color is used for baby girls. (Color symbolism used in other societies, religions, and mystical traditions may ascribe different colors to male and female infants. If you come from a different societal background or feel more comfortable with a different tradition, go ahead and use the colors appropriate to that system.)

This spell is best performed if both partners are in agreement about wanting a girl child. Choose the date to perform this spell by calculating the best time for conception. You may also want to take into consideration various seasonal and astrological factors. This spell should be performed in the evening before going to bed

To perform this spell, use the ritual provided in chapter 1, improvise a ritual of your own, or just proceed by laying out the cards and doing the visualization and affirmation.

Meditation and Visualization

When ready, lay down the World. Both of you should place your right hands on the card and stand for a minute while meditating on your desire for a female child. Picture a cute little baby girl—soft, cuddly, and dressed in pink. Picture yourselves interacting with her as a baby and when she is living through her formative years. Picture the feminine activities she'll likely participate in as she grows.

Lay down the Star and the Empress in turn, continuing the same visualizations.

At this point, it is time to take up the item, which you have chosen to use as a charm. Both of you should press the charm to the mother's abdomens while saying together the following affirmation.

Affirmation

"We call upon all good and helpful powers!

Hear us and aid us now,

for we desire a baby girl!

We are ready to love our little girl.

We are ready to provide a comfortable home for our daughter.

We are ready to make the greatest commitment to her.

This small item is a token of the commitment

that we are ready to make.

So it is, and so it shall be!"

Place the charm back by the card layout for the time being, and seal the spell with hugs and kisses, followed by the other necessary actions. You may consider the spell closed at this point, or you may close the spell as suggested in the rite in chapter 1, or as desired.

28. To encourage the conception of a baby boy.

*I*n this spell, the Sun is the focal card, representing the desired baby boy. Although there are no cards that are specifically meant to represent boys, the Sun usually refers to children in general. Here you can meditate on the picture of the child depicted in the Sun, emphasizing the connection between the words "Sun" and "son" in your mind. (If you have a deck which has a picture of two children on the Sun card, and you are afraid this will suggest having twins, and you don't want to have twins, then substitute whichever Page card appeals to you.) Also, in addition to depicting the father's role, the Emperor represents the principle of masculinity. The Ace of Wands is a card that can also represent the procreative force and the start of new life.

Note: I tend to be leery about trying to influence the sex of unborn children, since I feel that there may be karmic reasons for certain persons to be born to certain parents, and that a child's soul should choose the sex with which it can best express itself. However, I realize that having children of a certain sex can be very important to some parents, and have designed this spell in recognition of this need.

As an accessory for this spell, obtain one small baby boy's item to be used as a charm and to be included near your Tarot card layout. Anything that can be handled during the meditation will do: a blue rattle or other masculine baby toy, a layette item, and a family heirloom baby item, etc. The item chosen should be something that makes you feel good by just looking at it. Since this is also something that you will want to present to your newborn child, you should make sure that there is nothing in its contents or construction that could harm a baby.

If you wish to use other accessories for this spell, blue candles, flowers, crystals and gemstones, and cloth to lay the cards upon can be used, as in our society this color is used for baby boys. (Color symbolism used in other societies, religions, and mystical traditions may ascribe different colors to male and female infants. If you come from a different societal background or feel more comfortable with a different tradition, go ahead and use the colors appropriate to that system.)

This spell is best performed if both partners are in agreement about wanting a male child. Choose the date to perform this spell by calculating the best time for conception. You may also want to take into consideration various seasonal and astrological factors. This spell should be performed in the evening before going to bed.

To perform this spell, use the ritual provided in chapter 1, improvise a ritual of your own, or just proceed by laying out the cards and doing the meditation, visualization, and affirmation.

Meditation and Visualization

When ready, lay down the Sun. Both of you should place your right hands on the card and stand for a moment while meditating very strongly on the desire for a male child. Picture a little baby boy, dressed in blue. Picture yourselves interacting with him as a baby and throughout his formative years. Picture the masculine activities he'll likely participate in as he grows.

Lay down the Emperor and the Ace of Wands in turn, continuing the same visualizations. At this point, it is time to take up the item, which you have chosen to use as a charm. Both of you should press the charm to the mother's abdomen while saying together the following affirmation.

Affirmation

"We call upon all good and helpful powers!

Hear us and aid us now,

for we desire a baby boy!

We are ready to love our little boy.

We are ready to provide a comfortable home for our son.

We are ready to make the greatest commitment to him.

This small item is a token of the commitment

that we are ready to make.

So it is, and so it shall be!"

Place the charm back by the card layout for the time being, and seal the spell with hugs and kisses, followed by the other necessary actions.

You may consider the spell closed at this point, or you may close the spell as suggested in the rite in chapter 1, or as desired.

Competition

29. For success when faced with strong competition.

*T*here are certain jobs, fields, and other areas of life where competition seems to go with the territory. Some persons find competition stimulating and challenging; and others see no use for it and would prefer to have nothing to do with it. Whether you are among the former or the latter, this spell will help you stay on top of the competitive struggles that may arise in your life.

In this spell, a simple three-card layout makes a concise statement. The Five of Wands stands for struggle, here applied to competition. the Chariot stands for the ability to stay on top, and the Six of Wands for victory and success.

If you wish to use accessories for this spell, consider how you feel about situations where you are forced to compete. If you are a person who thrives on competition, use red or orange candles, flowers, crystals and gemstones, and cloth to lay the cards upon. Red stands for action and vitality; orange combines the same elements with intellectual energy. If, on the other hand, you find competition draining, use blue or green. Blue stands for calm and total relaxation, while green denotes healing and growth. If there are any tangible symbols of the struggles you face, include them near your card arrangement. For example: if you are a student entered in an essay contest, have your completed essay (or writing materials if incomplete) nearby as you work the spell.

To perform this spell, use the ritual provided in chapter 1, improvise a ritual of your own, or just proceed by laying out the cards and doing the meditation, visualization, and affirmation,

Meditation and Visualization

When ready, lay down the Five of Wands. Look closely at the picture on this card. Does the illustration suggest excitement to you, or does it provoke a weary feeling? Think about the competitive factors that you are dealing with; examine your attitudes about competition.

Next, set the Chariot in place. Ask yourself what is necessary to enable you to be on top of your competition. Would a new course of action do the trick, or do you simply need the energy and wit to persevere on your current path? Would a change of situation or environment help? Or is it a change in attitude that is needed? Now study the graphic symbolism of the Chariot. The charioteer is clearly a person in control of competing forces, Know that *you* have the power within you to be the charioteer. Envision yourself in whatever situation it is that you need to be in control of, exercising the mastery of the charioteer while at the same time maintaining his calm composure.

Finally, set the Six of Wands—the card of conquest—in place. Picture yourself in the future, enjoying the ideal culmination of your efforts, whether it be success, victory, achievement, or a peaceful retirement. Conjure up the feeling of elation that this would bring and savor it.

After you have finished meditating on the cards and visualizations, carefully, and with as much feeling as you can, recite the following affirmation.

Affirmation

"I call forth strength, wit, and skill

for great is the power within me!

I feel my power!

I know my power!

I assert my power!

I savor my power!

I go forth to meet all challenges

for I am the master (mistress) of all.

I am above it all.

I am calm and in control of all.

And all challenges bring me victory and success.

So it is, and so shall it be!"

You may consider the spell closed at this point, or you may close the spell as suggested in the rite in chapter 1, or as desired.

Courage

The Star   Strength   The Chariot

30. For courage in facing a difficult situation.

*T*he potential circumstances that require us to summon up courage are innumerable. Some are very frightening situations, and some are matters of great seriousness and importance. Others are just small things which give us trouble or which we want to put off for personal reasons. Whether the thing you fear is large or small, this spell will help.

This simple spell calls on the powers that will help you face any problem. The Star provides inner guidance, Strength gives courage and power, and the Chariot puts you in control of the situation.

If you wish to use accessories for this spell, try red candles, flowers, crystals and gemstones, and cloth to lay the cards upon. Red bestows the forceful energy needed to ride out a difficult period. You could also use brown, which denotes strength rooted in the Earth, or white, which stands for pure psychic energy and purity of intentions.

To perform this spell, use the ritual provided in chapter 1, improvise a ritual of your own, or just proceed by laying out the cards and doing the meditation, visualization, and affirmation.

Meditation and Visualization

When ready, lay down the Star. Visualize yourself standing in a field of stars. As you observe the stars, you notice their light becoming brighter and brighter. Beams of starlight extend to you, and you feel their warmth penetrating you, suffusing you with power. You become aware that you, too, are a glowing star, and you become intoxicated with the joy of your own light and power.

Next, set Strength in place. Continue to feel the vital energy, which you have summoned, and know that you have the power to overcome all fears and obstacles. Flex your muscles, and if your work space permits, engage in motions such as exercises, martial arts katas, or dance movements which make you aware of your body and being, and of the strength and energy that flow through you.

Finally, set the Chariot in place. Contemplate the figure in the picture; study his calm sense of control. Now, study the charioteer's armor. Using the psychic energy that you have summoned, you will craft your own protective armor: hold your hands in front of you, and feel the power surging through them. Now, starting with your head, make motions with your hands, passing them over your body parts, using their power to craft an invisible armored covering.

After you have finished meditating on the cards and visualizations, carefully, with as much feeling as you can, recite the affirmation.

Affirmation

"By force of will and magic spell
I call on power from within and without!
Power shines like a star within me.
Power flows through me,
and power grows 'round me.
I conjure power to make me strong.
With magic power I craft my armor.
My magic protects me totally
and no obstacle can stand before me.
In the warmth and light of my inner strength
fears and problems melt like snow.
So it is, and so shall it be!"

You may consider the spell closed at this point, or you may close the spell as suggested in the rite in chapter 1, or as desired.

Decisions

31. For help in making the best decision.

*T*his is a spell that you can use when you are having trouble making a decision, either because you have potentially conflicting choices or because you have so many options to choose from that you don't know which is the best.

The three-card layout is simple, making a concise statement: the subject wants the inner and outer guidance necessary to make the best decision and choose the best path to take.

The first card, the Star, stands for intuition and inner wisdom and guidance. The Hermit brings hidden knowledge to light (including options that you may have been unaware of), making clear the paths that lie before you. Justice stands for the ability to make carefully considered decisions.

If you wish to use accessories for this spell, use white candles, flowers, crystals and gemstones, and cloth to lay the cards upon. White stands for purity of motive and pure psychic energy.

Prior to performing this spell, write down the different choices that you are forced to make or the different options that you must consider. Make a list of pros and cons for each choice. (If you plan to do this spell for another person, it is best that he or she make up the list in advance.) Keep this list nearby when you arrange the Tarot cards. It is best to do this spell at night, before going to bed, so that your subconscious mind can have time to work on the problem.

To perform the spell, you may use the ritual provided in chapter 1, improvise a ritual of your own, or just proceed by laying out the cards and doing the following meditation, visualization, and affirmation.

Meditation and Visualization

When ready, lay down the Star in the position indicated in the diagram. Close your eyes and try to clear everything from your mind. Feel that you are in tune with that still, small voice within. Know that there's a Cosmic Consciousness out there, and that if you listen you can hear and can get help from hidden sources.

Next, lay down the Hermit. Take up the list of pros and cons which you have made, and consider the paths you have before you. Visualize all of the different options and what sort of consequences they would logically lead to.

Set Justice in place, knowing that the right decision will be made. Perhaps it is not possible to see that decision at this time, but know that the correct option, the correct path to take, will be revealed. All will be carefully considered, all the necessary information will be made available, all will be weighed, and the correct decision will be made.

After you have finished meditating on the cards and visualizations, carefully, and with as much feeling as you can, recite the following affirmation.

Affirmation

"I draw on the powers above me
and the powers within me!
I choose from the paths
which lay before me.
I balance all factors,
and weigh this problem.
Everything that I need to know
and every path which I need to take
is revealed to me.
All is in keeping with the longings of my heart and
the high destiny that I was born to.
So it is and so it shall be!"

You may consider the spell closed at this point, or you may close the spell as suggested in the rite in chapter 1, or as desired.

After you have completed the spell, put your question or questions out of your mind and think of them no further. Go to bed, but do not allow yourself to go over your problems as you fall asleep—leave that job to your unconscious mind. When you wake up the next morning, immediately take up a pen and paper and write down any impressions or ideas pertaining to the decision which you must make.

If you draw a blank, do not worry or strain your mind for ideas. Just put the matter out of your mind once again and go about your daily work. Allow the solution to come to you naturally. This may be revealed within a few days and may come to you in some unexpected moment. Just be patient and allow the spell to take its course. In short order you'll have a clear, firm idea of which decision to make, and which path to take.

You may consider the spell closed at this point, or you may close the spell as suggested in the rite in chapter 1, or as desired.

32. For help in sticking with a difficult decision.

*T*his spell lends aid when you have made a decision that you know is right for you but that may be tough to carry through, either because others will oppose it, or because you yourself need extra courage and resolve to carry it out.

The card pattern is concise and makes a strong but simple statement. Justice is the focal card, and represents you, carefully considering your decision and deliberating on the action you need to take. (If you want to make this layout more personal, you can choose a Significator card for yourself and place it superimposed over the Justice card, or vice versa, depending upon what appeals to you. Refer to appendix 1 if you need to know more about choosing a Significator.) The focal card is flanked by the Nine of Wands, depicting your ability to defend your decision, and the Chariot, depicting your ability to stay in control and on course after having made your resolution.

Note: The Strength card can be substituted for the Chariot or the Nine of Wands if it has greater appeal to you.

If you wish to use accessories for this spell, there are a variety of colors you can choose for flowers, candles, crystals and gemstones, cloth to lay the cards upon, and other accessories. You can use white to represent purity of motive. If you feel the main shortcoming in carrying out your plans is lack of energy, use red or orange. If the decision is an especially grave one and you are worried about obstacles and opposition use brown, which represents the steadfastness of the Earth, or black, which represents firm and somber resolve.

Prior to performing this spell, make a list of all the reasons why your decision is a good and necessary one. Keep this list nearby when you arrange the Tarot cards for the spell.

This is a spell that you would most likely perform shortly after having made a very difficult decision, particularly if you know that your decision is going to meet with a lot of opposition. If you know that on a particular day you are going to encounter the persons or things which will present the major obstacles to your resolve, perform this spell on that morning before going out.

To perform the spell, you may use the ritual provided in chapter 1, improvise a ritual of your own, or just proceed by laying out the cards and doing the following meditation, visualization, and affirmation.

Meditation and Visualization

When ready, lay down the Justice card. Then, pick up your list of reasons to carry through with your decision and read them slowly, again giving careful consideration to each reason.

Next, lay down the Nine of Wands to the left of Justice, as indicated in the diagram. Visualize yourself having the courage and ability to defend your decisions, holding firm against all potential opposition.

Now, lay down the Chariot. Visualize yourself going through the motions necessary to carry out your decision. Know that you have the strength needed to maintain control, and that you will persevere and triumph over all opposition.

After you have finished meditating on the cards and visualizations, carefully, and with as much feeling as you can, recite the following affirmation.

Affirmation

"The decision I have made is good.

The decision I have made is steadfast.

I am prepared to defend and carry out my decision.

I act from knowledge

I act from experience.

I act from strength.
I call upon the powers above me
I call upon the powers within me
to help me carry out my decision.
I am persistent.
I am steadfast in my purpose.
I am in control.
So it is, and so shall it be!"

You may consider the spell closed at this point, or you may close the spell as suggested in the rite in chapter 1, or as desired.

Divorce

33. To achieve an amicable divorce.

*D*ivorce is seldom painless, but when you have come to the point at which you feel it is the best solution, this spell will help ease the breakup.

Here, the central card is the Two of Cups, which grants a continued harmonious relationship, even though the two individuals are essentially in opposition. The Nine of Pentacles and the Eight of Cups, representing the wife and husband respectively, are arranged to show both parties achieving independence and self-sufficiency in a separation and departure which is for the best.

It would be well if the separating couple could perform this spell together. However, since this would probably be too painful for most divorcing persons to perform together, it is written to be performed by one alone. If both of you are willing to work this spell together, adjust the words and actions as necessary.

For this spell, prepare two identical goblets or cups with water or wine and set them near the card arrangement. If you wish to use other accessories for this spell, there are a variety of colors you can choose for flowers, candles, crystals and gemstones, cloth to lay the cards upon, and other accessories. You can use white to represent purity of motive, green for emotional healing, or blue for honesty, loyalty, and peace. To lend additional focus to the spell, you can place your wedding ring, other momentos of your marriage, and your divorce papers (if already drawn up) near the card arrangement.

In order to assure a minimum of strife while going through the divorce process, it is helpful to perform this spell as soon as the decision to divorce has been made.

To perform the spell, you may use the ritual provided in chapter 1, improvise a ritual of your own, or just proceed by laying out the cards and doing the following meditation, visualization, and affirmation.

Meditation and Visualization

When ready, lay down the Two of Cups, then take the two goblets you have prepared and set them, touching each other, just above the Two of Cups card. Visualize the good times you and your spouse shared. Spend several moments summoning up good memories of your relationship. Then, visualize yourself and your soon-to-be former partner working out the divorce, cooperating in a congenial, businesslike manner.

Next, set the Nine of Pentacles and the Eight of Cups down, one after the other, as indicated in the diagram. Picture yourself and the other party going off in opposite directions, leading fulfilled yet separate and independent lives. At this point, move the two goblets to opposite ends of the card layout area.

Now, take another look at the focal card, the Two of Cups. Once again, picture the two of you continuing to cooperate throughout the divorce and, where necessary, in the future.

After you have finished meditating on the cards and visualizations, carefully, and with as much feeling as you can, recite the following affirmation.

Affirmation

"With these cards and with this spell
I craft a good and harmonious future.
Though our paths shall separate,
(spouse's name) and I maintain
friendship and cooperation.
All is well.
All is in balance.
We are finding our own lives,
we are going our own ways richer for the experience.
Our lives continue to be whole
and healthy.
So it is, and so it shall be!"

You may consider the spell closed at this point, or you may close the spell as suggested in the rite in chapter 1, or as desired.

Note: Afterwards you may empty the contents of the goblets outdoors as a libation to Nature. If possible, empty each goblet in an opposite direction, or in a different quarter of your yard.

✶ ✳

Significator

Justice

11   11

Judgement

20   20

9

2

8

34. For a favorable divorce settlement.

*W*hen divorce seems to be the answer to your problems, this spell will help things work out in your best interest.

This spell elaborates on the layout for the previous spell (for amicable divorce), but adds legal elements and judgments. The Two of Cups provides the base that grants a continued harmonious relationship, even though the two individuals are essentially in opposition. The Nine of Pentacles and the Eight of Cups are part of a graphic division, representing the wife and husband respectively. They are arranged to show both partners achieving independence and self-sufficiency in a separation and departure that is for the best. Justice and Judgement are in the middle of the pyramid, denoting the legal processes. Justice represents the involvement of the legal system and the decisions that have to be made, and Judgement represents the favorable judgment that will result. Auspiciously, Judgement also stands for a renewed and revitalized life. Your Significator tops the pyramid, reinforcing the statement that all will work out in your favor.

Note: If you wish, you may use the World at the top of the pyramid, either as your Significator, or place it above or below your Significator. The World signifies the best of all possible outcomes.

If you wish to use accessories for this spell, use white flowers, candles, crystals and gemstones, and cloth to lay the cards upon, to signify purity of intentions, or gold and/or green to signify success and a good material and financial settlement. To lend additional focus to the spell, you can place your wedding ring, other mementos of your marriage, and any divorce papers already drawn up near the card arrangement.

In order to assure a minimum of strife while going through the divorce process, perform this spell as soon as the decision to divorce has been made.

To perform the spell, you may use the ritual provided in chapter 1, improvise a ritual of your own, or just proceed by laying out the cards and doing the following meditation, visualization, and affirmation.

Meditation and Visualization

When ready, turn to the spell just before this one (for an amicable divorce) for instructions and visualizations to go with the laying down of the first three cards, the Two of Cups, Nine of Pentacles, and Eight of Cups, which form the base of the pyramid. These cards are to ensure harmony and cooperation throughout the divorce process—qualities that are certainly necessary for obtaining a favorable settlement.

After you have done the visualizations for the Two of Cups, Nine of Pentacles, and Eight of Cups, set Justice in place, as indicated in the diagram. Now, visualize as best you can the legal actions that will have to be taken and the people who will be involved in the legal process. Picture all of these things working together to result in the best settlement for you.

Next, set Judgement in place, as indicated in the diagram. Picture yourself in court, hearing the judge's decision, and being very satisfied with the outcome. Picture the result of the judgment being what you need to start a new and revitalized life.

Finally, set your Significator in place. Now, try to visualize the "big picture," the combined effect of all of the images you have already visualized, with everything working out to enable you to live in peace, prosperity, and wholeness.

After you have finished meditating on the cards and visualizations, carefully, and with as much feeling as you can, recite the following affirmation.

Affirmation

"The cards that I place in patterns here
reflect what is, and what shall be.
Though our paths separate,
(spouse's name) and I maintain
cooperation and harmony.
(spouse's name) agrees to my wishes.
The legal procedures go smoothly,
and all goes well for me.
The judgement is good.
Everything works out fairly,
and I am content.
So it is, and so shall it be!"

You may consider the spell closed at this point, or you may close the spell as suggested in the rite in chapter 1, or as desired.

✱ ✳

Dreams

35. To encourage good dreams.

*T*here are many scientists, psychologists, and philosophers who study the nature and function of dreams. Many theories have been put forth as to what dreams are, and often the proponents of these theories are in disagreement as to what dreams do for us. Surely, however, few of us will disagree with the idea that very good dreams have the power to leave us with a warm glow that stays with us and makes us feel good throughout the day. Here is a spell to encourage your fondest dreams to come to you and to stay with you.

The Moon is the focal card in this spell, for in mystical tradition Luna is the creator of dreams. In the Tarot, the Moon represents the unconscious mind, where dreams, visions, imaginings, emotions, and magic originate. In this layout, the Moon is bolstered by cards to stimulate dreams, which will allow a positive, creative expression of the lunar nature. On the left, the Ace of Cups affects the province of dreams by bestowing beauty and riches in the realm of emotions. The outcome is the Star—creativity, beauty, and inspiration through dreams.

For this spell, it is necessary to have a silver, crystal, or other type of elegant goblet containing some clear water. If you wish to use other accessories for this dream spell, try blue candles; white flowers or flowers in soft, cool shades (pastel lavender, green, blue); and gemstones in soft shades, such as moonstones, aquamarines, and crystals. In addition, if you have a small silver or crystal charm, or some other object in the shape of the Moon or a star, keep it near the card layout. (A special silver coin would also be appropriate; this is also a traditional Moon symbol.) During the spell, this object can be charged with power and used as a charm to keep near your bed to inspire good dreams.

Although one would think that the best time for performing this spell is just before going to bed, I recommend against it. I have found that the best way to bring something out in dreams is to submit it to the unconscious mind and then forget about it. The mind has a very funny way of bringing suppressed ideas out in dreams. Therefore, I recommend performing this spell only once, and in the morning or sometime during the day. During the part of the spell where you do certain visualizations, meditate on the images only briefly—just long enough to make the complete picture. After performing the spell, immediately occupy yourself with some interesting activities to take your mind off the object of the spell.

To perform the spell, you may use the ritual provided in chapter 1, improvise a ritual of your own, or just proceed by laying out the cards and doing the following meditation, visualization, and affirmation.

Meditation and Visualization

When ready, lay down the Moon. If you have a charm that you want to charge, lay it on top of the Moon card. Now, visualize yourself standing under a moonlit sky. Sense the Moon as a nearby, kindly presence. Imagine that you see the Moon take on the shape of a beautiful shining lady with a crown of stars. Know that she is the Queen of Night and will send beautiful dreams to you.

Next, set the Ace of Cups in place to the left of the Moon. Now, imagine that the Moon Goddess is presenting you with a chalice containing a magical elixir, which will give you wondrous, happy dreams. At this point, take up the goblet, which you have prepared in advance and drink from it. Know that the drink you have prepared has indeed been transformed into the magical elixir through the power of your inner magic.

Finally, set the Star in place. Visualize yourself still standing under the moonlit sky, discovering that the potion you have drunk enables you to float up into the sky and drift freely among the glistening stars. Know that each of the beautiful stars surrounding you will bestow on you a special dream. Briefly consider what type of dream adventures would make you happiest.

End the visualization when you feel that it is complete. After you have finished meditating on the cards and visualizations, recite the following affirmation.

Affirmation

"I have tasted the magical elixir
which brings dreams of inspiration and wonder.
Every night as I sleep,
my spirit is drawn into realms
of beauty and light.
Magic, romance, and enchantment
shine through my nighttime dreams
and linger with me when I wake.
This magic is
and this magic shall be!"

You may consider the spell closed at this point, or you may close the spell as suggested in the rite in chapter 1, or as desired. If there's any left you can finish the drink, if you like.

36. For prophetic dreams.

*P*erhaps the most extraordinary dreams we can experience are those that allow us to see into the future. Through this spell, hidden knowledge of the future is revealed in dreams and brought out into the light.

The first card in this layout is the High Priestess, the guardian of hidden wisdom and knowledge of the future. This card influences the focal card, the Moon, ruler of dreams, to inspire prophetic visions. The hermit symbolizes the desire to uncover truth, and his lamp brings the knowledge hidden in dreams to light.

An unlit lantern, lamp, or candle will be a necessary accessory for this spell. Also, have nearby some matches or whatever is necessary to light your lamp with. If you decide to use a candle, you may have this in addition to the other candles that are called for if you decide to do the ritual in chapter 1. If you wish to use additional accessories for this dream spell, try blue candles; white flowers or flowers in soft, cool shades (pastel lavender, green, blue), and gemstones such as moonstones, aquamarines, and crystals in soft shades. In addition, if you have a small silver or crystal charm or some other object in the shape of the Moon or a star, keep it near the card layout. A crystal or gemstone can be used for this purpose too, and a special silver coin would also be appropriate (this is also a traditional Moon symbol). During the spell, this object can be charged with power to be used as a charm to keep near your bed to inspire prophetic dreams.

As with the previous spell, I recommend performing this spell only once, and in the morning or sometime during the day. During the part of the spell where you do certain visualizations, meditate on the images only briefly, just long enough to make the complete picture. After performing the spell, immediately occupy yourself with some interesting activities to take your mind off of the object of the spell.

To perform the spell, you may use the ritual provided in chapter 1, improvise a ritual of your own, or just proceed by laying out the cards and doing the following meditation, visualization, and affirmation.

Meditation and Visualization

For this spell, it will be necessary to lay the cards out from right to left and from bottom to top. When ready, lay down the Hermit, For your meditation, visualize yourself standing on a vast plain beneath a moonlit sky. In your visualization, you take up an unlit lamp, and hold it up to the sky. A moonbeam falls across the lamp, and then, suddenly, within the lamp a star begins to take shape. In actuality, pick up your lantern or candle at this point, and light it. Close your eyes for a short space, and try to hold the image of the lamplight burning in your mind.

Next, set the Moon in place, up to the left of the Hermit, as indicated in the diagram. Notice the symbolism in the artwork, and how the lamp of the Hermit is held up to the Moon. If you have a charm that you want to charge, lay it on top of the Moon card at this point. In your continued visualization you see, by the light of the lamp, that a path is stretching on before you. You follow the path as the Moon above looks down on you. Your path leads down to a river, where a shrouded man in a boat is waiting for you. Without exchanging any words, you get into the boat and he ferries you across to the other side. The path starts up again, and you continue to follow it until you come to a gateway between two towers.

Set the High Priestess in place, above and to the left of the Moon as indicated in the diagram. In your continued visualization you pass through the gate and find yourself facing a temple. Entering the temple, you see a throne between two pillars.

On the throne is a scroll. You do not open the scroll at this time, but you are aware that if you open the scroll, images of the future will begin to appear and will grow larger and larger, taking on a three-dimensional form. The images will become so real that it will seem to you that you are actually present in these future scenarios, an invisible witness to the action taking place. Know that you are the High Priestess (or Priest), and that from here on you will be able to return to this place in your dreams, and that at such times you will open the scroll and get glimpses of the future.

End the visualization at this point. After you have finished meditating on the cards and visualizations, recite the following affirmation.

Affirmation

"I call upon the mystical light of the Moon

and the magical light of the stars!

Shine through my dreams

and bring hidden knowledge to light.

I follow the path of wisdom

and I can see all that lies before me.

Visions of the future are revealed to me.

The meaning of the future is made clear to me.

So it is, and so shall it be!"

You may consider the spell closed at this point, or you may close the spell as suggested in the rite in chapter 1, or as desired.

Emotions

37. For cheerfulness, good moods, and a positive outlook.

*T*his is a spell to lift your spirits and give you a fresh outlook on life. Whether you have been under deep emotional strain, are feeling a bit blue, or just want to enhance the quality of your emotional life, these magical images will give you a boost by surrounding you with positive thought-forms.

This layout takes the shape of the life rune to signify "reaching up" to the possibilities that life has to offer, with emotions and spirits being uplifted. Your Significator is superimposed over the Moon. The Moon represents the emotional nature; having the Significator on top of it depicts your own emotional nature, and it also symbolizes your asserting control over the emotions. Your Significator is flanked by the Ace of Cups for emotional riches and the Sun for happiness. It is crowned by the World, representing harmony and wholeness.

A particularly nice glass or goblet filled with water is a necessary accessory for this spell. For additional accessories that will magnify the uplifting effect of this spell, choose flowers, candles, crystals and gemstones, and cloth to lay the cards upon, in shades of pink, rose, or yellow. Pink and rose emanate cheerful well-being—"being in the pink." Yellow radiates cheerfulness and hopefulness. If you plan to do this spell for someone other than yourself, you will want to include something belonging to that person near the card layout.

This spell may be performed at anytime, but it is most auspicious to perform it on the morning of a day that you have designated as a day of new beginnings. Afterwards, you may wish to do an abbreviated version of this spell each morning in order to keep its power going strong.

To perform this spell, you may use the ritual provided in chapter 1, improvise a ritual of your own, or just proceed by following the directions given here, laying out the cards and doing the meditation, visualization, and affirmation.

Meditation and Visualization

When ready, set the Moon in place, as indicated on the diagram. Consider how the Moon is considered to be the ruler of emotions. Astrologically, it controls the emotional tides. Think back on the times that you have had emotional highs that made you feel powerful and expansive. Relive these feelings.

Set the Significator on top of the Moon, covering it. Think of your emotional being. Think about how you would feel and what you could accomplish if you could summon an emotional high whenever you needed it.

Set the Ace of Cups in place to the left of the Significator. This is the sign of emotional richness. At this point, take up the glass or goblet you have prepared. Go to the window, and catch some sunlight in your glass (or, if at night, moonlight). Drink the water while visualizing yourself (or the subject, if you are doing this for someone else) drinking a special brew that will have an intoxicating effect. The magical elixir makes you happy, cheerful, and ebullient—like a drug—but a very healthy one! (If it is not possible to get sunlight or moonlight to touch your goblet, just imagine yourself standing out under the Sun, doing this.)

Next, set down the World. Picture your world in balance, your life in harmony with your surroundings. Picture yourself going about your day, energized by a positive outlook.

Lastly, set down the Sun. Picture yourself basking in the glow of the Sun, feeling the warmth, feeling good all over, and knowing that you can maintain your positive outlook. Picture yourself spreading your arms, saying, "I am here! I am I! All is wonderful!" Know that whenever you see the Sun or one of its symbols, you will re-experience this expansive feeling. (Later you may place Sun symbols around your home and place of work to reinforce this spell.) If you are doing this spell for another person, take up their personal object at this point, and warm it in your hands, visualizing it being filled with the warmth of the Sun.

After you have finished meditating on the cards and visualizations, carefully, and with as much feeling as you can, recite the following affirmation.

Affirmation

"From the depths of my soul
to the heights of all that exists,
my joy rises!
I drink the elixir of happiness
and my world is filled with delight.
All is right with the world,
and the world is right with me!
The Moon brings me sweet emotions,
and the Sun shines on me wherever I go!
So it is,
and so shall it be!"

You may consider the spell closed at this point, or you may close the spell as suggested in the rite in chapter 1, or as desired.

Note: For an alternative spell to accomplish this goal, go through the Tarot deck and pick out the cards with symbols to which you have an especially strong positive response. (In other words, the cards that make you feel good.) Lay down the Moon and place your Significator card on top of it; then use the other cards you've chosen to encircle it, making a mandala or a wheel-shaped layout with your Significator in the center.

38. To purge oneself of old emotional pain and guilt.

Negative emotions, unhappy memories, and guilt have an ability to drain our energy and prevent us from living life to its fullest. If such emotions have been limiting you, this spell will help you make a positive transformation.

This layout shows the process of purging anxiety-causing emotions and transforming their negative energies into positive strengths. Here the Moon, ruler of the emotions, is used to denote the tortuous emotions that have been troubling you. Judgement denotes your will to purify and transform your emotional being. The World represents your perfected self, living in a state of harmony and grace.

For this spell, a white candle is a necessary accessory, as well as some sort of a fireproof vessel, such as a large brazier. Also have at hand a piece of clean white paper and a pencil or pen. If you wish to use additional accessories, use white flowers, crystals, and gemstones, and cloth to lay the cards upon. The white symbolizes purified emotions.

To perform this spell, you may use the ritual provided in chapter 1, improvise a ritual of your own, or just proceed by following the directions given here, laying out the cards and doing the meditation, visualization, and affirmation.

Meditation and Visualization

When ready, light the white candle. Then, by the light of the candle, list the memories and emotions that have been troubling you. Take as much time and thought as you need to write down these feelings.

Next, lay down the Moon. As you lay down the Moon, think of the painful words you have written. Think of the burden that these unhealthy emotions have created for you. Realize that you must release the past, for the past cannot be changed, and such useless guilty emotions only rob you of your own power.

As you consider your desire to be free of such tortuous feelings, crumple the paper that you have written on, hold it to the candle so that it catches fire, and drop it into the fireproof howl or brazier.

As you watch the paper burning to ashes, set down Judgement, considering the depiction of metamorphosis and rebirth illustrated in this card. Imagine yourself calling upon the power within you to summon a flame that purges your being. It is a magical fire that causes you no pain, but rather causes you to feel invigorated. Dispassionately, you watch the flame transform you as it consumes all within you that hinders, harms, and makes guilty.

Finally, set the World in place. Know that you have taken back the energy that your painful memories had stolen from you, and you have used your own power to purge and transform yourself into a being of light—playful, strong, and free! The radiance that flows from you imbues everything around you with light and love.

After you have finished meditating on the cards and visualizations, carefully, and with as much feeling as you can, recite the following affirmation.

Affirmation

"I call upon the cosmic forces
and the power that burns within me!
I release old guilt.
I release old troubles.
All which is old and outworn,
All which gives pain,
All which gives anguish,
is consumed by the flame that
I have summoned and is no more.
I herewith call forth the powers of light,
and love, and laughter
to fill my being with radiance!
I dance and play in the light of the Sun
a free and joyous spirit!
So it is, and so it shall be!"

You may consider the spell closed at this point, or you may close the spell as suggested in the rite in chapter 1, or as desired.

Enemies

39. To discourage a pest from coming around.

We are all familiar with the many varieties of human pests: those who irritate you by their very presence, those who harass you, those who want something from you, and those who just want to eat up your time. This spell is used to nudge the pest away, turning him or her in another direction to, hopefully, follow higher pursuits.

In this simple, straightforward layout, the Two of Swords bars the pest's path and access to you. The Ace of Swords depicts the strong forces that you summon to drive the pest away. The Eight of Cups shows the pest forced to give up and go off in another direction. (There is a certain biblical symbolism in the combination of these cards, reminiscent of the angel driving Adam and Eve out of Eden with a fiery sword.)

As an accessory for this spell, have a sharp knife near your card layout. (A double-edged blade is ideal.) Other accessories can include black candles, crystals and gemstones, and cloth to lay the cards upon. Black is good for protective spells of this nature, for it stands for impenetrability.

To perform this spell, you may use the ritual provided in chapter 1, improvise a ritual of your own, or just proceed by following the directions given here, laying out the cards and doing the meditation, visualization, and affirmation.

Meditation and Visualization

When ready, set the Two of Swords in place. Take up the knife. Sense that psychic energy is flowing through your arm into the knife. With the knife, inscribe a large "X" in the air in front of you. Imagine that you have built an invisible force field that will prevent any nuisance from coming near you. Now, visualize yourself at home, in the office, or wherever it is that you are most likely to be approached by the pest. Visualize the pest coming toward you, only to find him or her rebuffed by an invisible wall. The pest keeps trying to get past the barrier, but is unable to.

Next, lay the Ace of Swords in place. Take the knife, and touch its point to the point of the sword in the card. Resume the visualization, picturing the pest still unable to move forward and now feeling intensely uncomfortable, as if a fiery sword were pointed at him or her, prodding him or her to turn away and retreat.

Finally, set the Eight of Cups in place. Picture the pest directing his or her energies toward a new activity or interest, in a different place. Picture the pest following his or her new goal, with back turned to you, heading off toward the horizon.

After you have finished meditating on the cards and visualizations, hold the knife over the card layout and carefully, and with as much feeling as you can, recite the following affirmation.

Affirmation

"With cards and knife

this spell is set in motion!

(Name of pest) is unable to move forward.

(Pest) cannot come near me.

(Pest) feels great discomfort.

(Pest) is driven away.

(Pest) is seen no more.

(Pest) has gone far away,

away to something better.

So it is, and so shall it be!"

You may consider the spell closed at this point, or you may close the spell as suggested in the rite in chapter 1, or as desired.

Significator

40. To restrain the actions of a malicious person.

*A*lthough we acknowledge that each person shares a spark of the Divine, and is therefore worthy of being loved and honored, most of us are all too aware that there are persons whose negative energies and destructive actions have a harmful effect on others. If such an individual is troubling you, this spell offers protection from both physical and psychic forms of harm. It utilizes a bell-jar technique, shielding you and deflecting your foe's ill will back to its source. Your adversary is restrained by being sealed within a magical container, causing him or her to stew in his or her own juices.

The cross-shaped layout serves a dual purpose here. The cross is an ancient symbol of protection, and here it shields you from the person who would harm you. At the same time, cards that form the arms of the cross act as wards to restrain the destructive individual in question.

In this particular spell, the subject or Significator is the person who needs to be restrained (rather than the person who is performing the spell). If you can't think of an appropriate Significator to use for your adversary, or if this is a case where the identity of the person is unknown to you, it would be acceptable to use the Devil in the central position. If that seems too intense, you could instead use the King, Queen, Knight, or Page of Swords, as these cards sometimes represent adversaries. (For more information, refer to appendix 1, "Significators".)

The Two of Swords, Hanged Man, and Eight of Swords show your would-be troublemaker plagued by indecision, unable to move, and forced to give up his or her malicious plans or actions. Temperance tops the layout to encourage this person to use some self-restraint, too, and can also represent the protective powers of good spirits and energies preventing this person from doing harm.

Note: If the situation that has made it necessary for you to do this spell requires the intervention of the law, substitute Justice for Temperance. If government intervention is needed, substitute the Emperor for Temperance.

A necessary accessory for this spell is a glass jar. It can be as plain or fancy as you please. Also, try to obtain a photo, some personal possession, or an object that has come in contact with your adversary. The object must be small enough to be fitted into the jar. If this is not possible, simply provide a piece of paper with his or her name on it. If yours is a hidden rival or opponent whose name you do not know, then take a piece of paper and write down what you do know of the person and situation that is causing you problems.

If you wish to use additional accessories, you may use candles, flowers, crystals and gemstones, and cloth to lay the cards upon in white to represent the purity of your intentions, or black to represent the impenetrable barrier you plan to put between yourself and the destructive individual in question.

To perform this spell, you may start by performing the ritual provided in chapter 1, improvise a ritual of your own, or just proceed by following the directions given here, laying out the cards and doing the meditation, visualization, and affirmation.

Meditation and Visualization

When ready, set the Significator in place, thinking about the person who has been creating problems for you as you do so. If you have an object that has come in contact with that person, pick it up briefly as you think about the person and the problem. (Or use the piece of paper with the name or situation written on it, as mentioned earlier.) Then, if the object is small enough, it can be laid on top of the Significator card.

Next, in quick succession, lay the Eight of Swords to the right of the Significator, the Hanged Man below it, the Two of Swords to the left, and Temperance above.

Immediately after placing these cards, take your hands and make a clockwise circle over the layout, starting with the Eight of Swords. Continue to make the circular motion, imagining power flowing from your hands and building a circle of power around these cards. As you do so, look at the symbolism on each card and envision your adversary being bound, blocked, confined and contained by the qualities of these cards.

When you feel you have put enough energy into the motions and visualizations, take the jar that you have prepared and place your enemy's photo, personal object or the piece of paper with the name or problem written on it in the jar. Seal the jar tightly.

Now, carefully, and with as much feeling as you can, recite the following affirmation.

Affirmation

"(Subject's name) is bound.

(Subject) is blocked.

(Subject) is confined.

(Subject) is unable to move.

(Subject) can do no harm.

Any negative energies that (subject) sends out

will be deflected back to him/her.

(Subject) will stew in his/her own juices

until he/she learns to do only good deeds

and send out only positive energies.

So it is, and so shall it be!"

You may consider the spell closed at this point, or you may close the spell as suggested in the rite in chapter 1, or as desired.

Put the jar away in a safe place. When, eventually, your problems with this individual are resolved, the objects may be taken out of the jar and casually disposed of.

Cleanse the card you used for the Significator by bathing it for a few moments in sunlight.

41. To undo and put right the actions of a malicious person.

*W*hereas the previous spell sought to protect the spellcaster from the actions of a malicious person, this spell is performed to mitigate damage that has already been done.

This more complex layout has the Devil coupled with Judgement to signify that the wrongdoing will be revealed and the necessary judgments and transformations will be set in motion, both to punish the perpetrator and to begin the process of repair. The Tower shows that the harm and evil already established will be undone and destroyed. In the aftermath, things are set right (Temperance) and harmony and well-being result (the World).

In advance of this spell, write down an account of the nature of the harm that has been done, and the motivations and actions of the person who has done it. Include this near your card layout. Also have a white candle and a brazier or some sort of large, fireproof bowl or vessel. If other accessories are desired, include white flowers, crystals and gemstones, and cloth to lay the cards upon. White symbolizes purity of intent and pure, vital energy directed toward purging and rebuilding.

To perform this spell, you may start by performing the ritual provided in chapter 1, improvise a ritual of your own, or just proceed by following the directions given here, laying out the cards and doing the meditation, visualization, and affirmation.

Meditation and Visualization

When ready, set the Devil and Judgement in place, as indicated on the diagram. Take up the piece of paper and reread your written account of the malicious person and the harm that has been done. Consider what sort of exposure, judgment, and rectification will be needed to start the process of healing, repair, and rebuilding in motion. Now, study the images on the cards, and know that as you do so, both magical and material channels are being opened to accomplish this work.

Next, set the Tower in place. As you consider the meaning of this card—the destruction of something which is corrupt—crumple the paper that you have written on, hold it to the candle so that it catches fire, and drop it into the fireproof bowl or brazier. Watch the paper burning to ashes.

Lastly, set Temperance and the World in place. Visualize a scenario where all the harm has been undone; all has been repaired, rebuilt, and set right; the malicious person has reformed and is now directing his or her energies toward doing positive and constructive things; and everything in your world is in harmony and balance.

After you have finished meditating on the cards and visualizations, carefully, and with as much feeling as you can, recite the following affirmation.

Affirmation

"With these cards and with this spell

Great and awesome forces are set in motion!

I summon, stir, and call upon the wide-ranging powers to work justice,

to work retribution,

to work repair,

to work transformation.

The evil that (subject's name) has done

is burned away to nothingness.

The channels for change are open.

Where hurt has been done,

there is now healing.

Where damage has been done,

there is now rebuilding.

Where slander has been done

there is now vindication.

All is in balance.

All is in harmony.

So it is, and so shall it be!"

You may consider the spell closed at this point, or you may close the spell as suggested in the rite in chapter 1, or as desired.

Families

42. For a truce in family quarrels.

All of us have experienced the stress and strain of divisive family quarrels at one time or another. Such conflicts can revolve around marital breakups, inheritances, adolescent rebellion, family business partnerships, etc. If you or other members of your family are currently caught up in some especially destructive dispute, perform this spell to promote fence-mending, peace, and healing.

This layout creates a sense of balance. In this spell, the Ten of Cups represents the family and is flanked by cards of compromise. The Two of Swords is especially appropriate where family quarrels have involved violence and bitterness. The Two of Cups recognizes that even where there is tension and competition, there can be balance and harmony.

As an accessory for this spell, have a goblet or chalice filled with a pleasant-tasting beverage such as sweet wine, fruit juice, milk, or pure water next to your card layout. If you wish to use other accessories for this spell, have pictures of the family, especially of the ones who are antagonists, set up around the card layout. If possible, include a picture showing the antagonists together in happier times. Also, include belongings of theirs, if you have them. For flowers, candles, crystals and gemstones, and cloth to lay the cards upon, use white to signify purity of intention, green for peace and healing, or pink for general well-being.

To perform this spell, you may use the ritual provided in chapter 1, improvise a ritual of your own, or just proceed by laying out the cards and doing the following meditation, visualization, and affirmation.

Meditation and Visualization

Before starting, spend some time handling and examining any pictures or personal belongings of family members that you may have on hand.

When ready, set down the Two of Swords in the position indicated on the diagram. Take the cup with your right hand, make a toasting gesture over the Two of Swords, and hold the cup over it while you visualize the feuding parties in your family. In your imagination, see them all becoming suddenly calm and peaceful, unable and unwilling to continue quarreling. Take a sip of the drink while you continue this visualization.

Next, set the Ten of Cups in place. Now make a toasting gesture and hold the cup over this card while you visualize your family members enjoying each other's company and sharing good times together, all quarrels now long forgotten. Take another sip of the drink while you continue this visualization.

Finally, set the Two of Cups down. Again, hold the cup over this card while you visualize a future where your family members are able to work together and get along despite individual disagreements and differences. Drink the rest of the beverage while continuing the visualization.

After you have finished meditating on the cards and visualizations, carefully, and with as much feeling as you can, recite the following affirmation.

Affirmation

"In these cards are reflected the images
of the reality which we now shape.
We are a family.
Peace is with us and peace is around us.
Where conflict has been,
there is compromise.
Where quarrels have been,
there is now understanding.
We share good times.
We share good memories.
We enjoy being together.
We enjoy working together.
We enjoy helping each other.
All is well in our family.
So it is, and so shall it be!"

You may consider the spell closed at this point, or you may close the spell as suggested in chapter 1, or as desired.

Significator

43. For a harmonious relationship with both parents.

*T*his spell is performed to help you develop your relationship with your parents. It can be used to help you learn to get along with your parents in the present. It can be used to make peace with conflicts from the past. Many of today's self-help books stress the need to forgive and come to terms with your parents in order to achieve healing, wholeness, and self-actualization. This spell will help with this process, whether it be dealing with your physical parents, or the images of the parents within you which are legacies in your subconscious.

This spell deals with relationships with your parents, so your Significator card is used in combination with those of your parents.

The balanced layout places it in a position relating to your parents and to the World, which represents happiness, wholeness, and harmony, peace and life. The Emperor and the Empress are used to represent the father and mother in the diagrams, as they typically denote parents. However, if you've already selected other Significator cards for your parents, you may use them in place of the Emperor and the Empress.

(This and the following two spells can also be adapted to your relationship with other relatives by substituting the Significator cards that you feel best represent the persons in question. For suggestions on choosing Significator cards, refer to appendix 1.)

Note that the Emperor, Empress, or any other Significator cards you choose to represent your parents or others should (when possible) be arranged so that they face each other and your own Significator. For example, in the Robin Wood deck the Empress faces left, so she is here placed on the right side of the layout, looking inward. If you are using another deck, check to see whether you might want to change the position of any of these cards.

If you wish to use accessories for this spell, have some pictures or small personal belongings of your parents near the area where the cards are to be laid out. As colors for candles, flowers, crystals and gemstones, and cloth to lay the cards upon, I suggest white for unity and purity of intention, pink for affection, green for healing emotional damage and the growth of a new relationship, or blue for peace and loyalty.

To perform this spell, you may use the ritual provided in chapter 1, improvise a ritual of your own, or just proceed by laying out the cards and doing the following meditation, visualization, and affirmation.

Meditation and Visualization

Because this spell seeks to establish unity and harmony among all those involved, set all the cards in place, one after another, in the position indicated in the diagram. (Note that this is unlike the other spells in this book in which there is a separate meditation and visualization for each card.) It does not matter which card you set down first.

Now, as you stand and gaze at the cards, think about your relationship with your mother and father: how it was when you were a small child, your parents' bad points, their good points, what you'd like to achieve, what you are willing to compromise on, what they need to compromise, how you all can make things better.

After thinking about these things for a while, take up the pictures or personal belongings of your parents, if you have them, and try to feel and experience through them your parents' personal energies and essence.

Next, put down the picture and belongings. Now, hold your right hand with your palm spread out wide over the card layout. Imagine that power is flowing through your arm and hand. Visualize that power taking on the color that you feel best symbolizes what you want to achieve (as mentioned in reference to accessories). Direct that color energy into the empty space in the center of your layout, and then let it flow outward in all directions, imbuing the other cards with colored light which circulates through them and binds them all together.

After you have finished meditating on the cards and visualizations, carefully, and with as much feeling as you can, recite the following affirmation.

Affirmation

"My world is filled with love

and peace

and harmony

Love and peace fill my inner being.

I let love and peace flow through me.

My relationships are a mirror of my inner harmony.

I am willing to change my relationship with my mother.

I forgive my mother.

I release the past.

I extend understanding and acceptance

and my mother responds to me

with understanding and acceptance.

I am willing to change my relationship with my father.

I forgive my father.

I release the past.

I extend understanding and acceptance

and my father responds to me

with understanding and acceptance.

My father, my mother, and I
are *one* in peace and harmony.
So it is, and so shall it be!"

You may consider the spell closed at this point, or you may close the spell as suggested in chapter 1, or as desired.

| | | Significator |

44. For a harmonious relationship with your father.

*P*erform this spell if you need to take the initiative in building a better relationship with your father.

In this simple three-card spread, the World acts as a bridge and a bond to create harmony and good feelings. Use the basic instructions, visualizations, etc., for the previous spell, but omit references to your mother and reword and make adaptations as necessary.

Significator

45. For a harmonious relationship with your mother.

*P*erform this spell if you need to improve your relationship with your mother. In this simple three-card spread, the World acts as a bridge and a bond to create harmony and good feelings. Use the basic instructions, visualizations, etc., of the spell for building a harmonious relationship with both parents, but omit references to your father and reword and make adaptations as necessary.

Farms and Gardens

46. For fertility of crops and general success in farming.

*T*his pyramidal layout symbolizes growth and upward movement. Note also the placement of the Sun and its significance to agriculture. The Empress is a card that denotes fertility in all things, including fertility of crops. The Seven of Pentacles suggests long-term projects, and can apply to agriculture literally as well as graphically. The Three of Cups represents harvest home and the celebration of bounty.

When using accessories for this spell, be sure to surround your layout with fresh flowers, as well as samples or seed packets of the varieties of fruits and vegetables that you raise or plan to raise. A picture of your farm or garden or the piece of property you plan to farm or garden on will also be a helpful prop. Other accessories can include green candles, green crystals and gemstones, and a green cloth to lay the cards upon.

To perform this spell, you may use the ritual provided in chapter 1, improvise a ritual of your own, or just proceed by laying out the cards according to the diagram and doing the following meditation, visualization, and affirmation.

Meditation and Visualization

Lay out the cards when you come to the appropriate point in the spell.

First, lay down the Sun, visualizing the Sun shining on your own farm or garden, sending its nourishing rays. Visualize your young and tender crops pushing up through the Earth to greet the Sun.

As you lay down the Empress, visualize the fertility that she represents—rain, mild weather, fertile soil.

Lay down the Seven of Pentacles, and visualize yourself working hard in your garden, enjoying the feel of the Sun and the feel of the soil as you do so. Imagine the anticipation that you will feel as you watch your crops ripening to maturity.

As you lay down the Three of Cups, visualize what your farm or garden will look like in full bloom, cultivated and with everything lushly growing. Picture yourself reaping your harvest, and feasting and celebrating afterward. Think of the sense of satisfaction that you will feel, knowing that your crops will bring security and plenty.

After meditating on these images for a while, pick up and handle the seeds or plant samples, envisioning power flowing into them as you stroke them.

After you have finished meditating on the cards and visualizations, carefully, and with as much feeling as you can, recite the following affirmation while placing your hand just above the cards and making a circle over them in a clockwise motion.

Affirmation

"I call upon the powers
of the Sun, the Earth,
the rain, and the soil!
My crops grow high!
The land prospers,
and all thereon grows strong,
and full, and rich!
This I do ask!
For my land and all upon it,
So be it!"

You may consider the spell closed at this point, or you may close the spell as suggested in the rite in chapter 1, or as desired.

Friends

Significator

Knight of Cups

47. To attract many friends.

*T*his spell is based on the principle that "like attracts like." Perform this spell if you want to expand your circle of friends and find other persons who share your interests—who are "kindred spirits."

The first card in this layout is a Knight. Knights represent new persons who come into your life and get you involved in new experiences. Choose the knight from the suit which best typifies your interests: Wands for active types, Cups for emotionally oriented persons, Swords for intellectuals, and Pentacles for trades and craftspersons. (For more on the personalities associated with the Knights, refer to appendix 1, "Choosing a Significator.") The Two of Cups covering your Significator is a bridge to a relationship between yourself and those others you would enjoy having enter your life. The Three of Cups shows the objective: you sharing good times with good friends.

As accessories for this spell, you will need two identical glasses or goblets. Choose the nicest ones you can find, perhaps buying some especially for this purpose. Have one of the goblets filled with pure water (or any other beverage that is pleasing to you), and set them near the area where the cards are to be laid out. (Also, have a napkin on hand, in case there are any spills.) If you wish other accessories, choose candles, flowers, crystals and gemstones, and cloth to lay the cards upon, in shades of blue for loyalty and friendship, white for purity of intention and the pure energy that can be converted into any shade of friendship, or gold for attractiveness and expansiveness.

To perform this spell, you may use it in combination with the ritual provided in chapter 1, improvise a ritual of your own, or just proceed by laying out the cards and doing the following meditation, visualization, and affirmation.

Meditation and Visualization

When ready, set your Significator down first. Visualize the kind of person you are, what you like to do, what sort of experiences you like to share with others.

Next set the Two of Cups in place on top of your Significator. Think about your need to reach out and connect with more people. You are a person who wants good friends, and who is also capable of being a good friend.

Now, to the left of this, set down the Knight—the one which you have chosen to represent your interests and the sort of things which you would like to become involved in. Consider how channels are opening to bring people into your life who will share your interests.

Finally, lay down the Three of Cups to the right, as indicated in the diagram. Visualize yourself enjoying yourself among other people in the type of setting that you most prefer. If you are an active sort who enjoys being out in nature, you might picture yourself among friends at the beach, on a hike, or at a picnic. If intellectual matters are more appealing to you, you might picture yourself at a soirée, holding stimulating discussions with interesting characters. Whatever activities you choose to visualize, hold their images in your mind for a few minutes.

After having devoted a few moments to the visualization, take up the two goblets and pour the fluid slowly and carefully from one cup to the other while saying the following affirmation.

Affirmation

"I reach out with the power of my heart,

and the power of my mind!

I call to those with kindred spirits,

hearts, and minds,

and they answer me.

I give friendship,

I take friendship.

I share good times with my friends.

All channels of society are open to me.

Friendship comes from many sources,

from near,

from far,

from expected sources,

and unexpected sources.

As I will,

so it is, and so shall it be!"

When you are finished with the affirmation, divide the fluid so there is an equal amount in each cup, and then take a sip from each cup. (You may drink it all, if you like.)

You may consider the spell closed at this point or you may close the spell as suggested in the rite in chapter 1, or as desired.

48. To attract influential friends to network for business purposes.

A person always needs contacts. This is a spell to open channels so that you can find friends, as well as friends' friends, that you can link up with for purposes of networking. ("Networking" means knowing people that can help you along, and that you, in turn, can also help along.) Everyone benefits by such relationships.

For this spell, simply alter the preceding spell. For accessories you may also use the color purple, which signifies high stations in life, and the generosity and nobility of the planet Jupiter (the king of the gods). For connections to achieve financial betterment, you may want to put more emphasis on the color gold. Or, perhaps, try using combinations of purple and gold.

On the right side of the layout, substitute the Ace of Pentacles for the Three of Cups if you want to emphasize the material and financial advantages you hope to gain by your new friendships, or substitute the Star if you want to invoke all-around good luck in choosing influential friends. When you do the visualization for the Ace of Pentacles or the Star, visualize yourself enjoying the prosperity as well as the social and emotional benefits that your new friendships will bring. Feel the sense of security resulting from knowing that you have friends, and that people care about you, that there are people you can count on when you need them.

For the affirmation, after you have said " . . . and unexpected sources," add:

"Our friendship brings prosperity to all,

we help each other,

and we all benefit thereby."

Then finish the affirmation and close the spell as directed.

Health and Healing

49. For all-around good health.

*G*ood health is one of the most desirable goals we can set for ourselves. This spell, in combination with a good program of care, nutrition, and exercise will speed you toward that goal.

This layout presents a picture of general well-being. Its shape is that of the life rune, the Old Norse charm, which is reminiscent of a figure with arms, outspread, drinking in life. The Magician is superimposed over the Significator to signify the subject's commitment to shape and improve his or her own personal health. These cards are crowned by the World, standing for health, harmony, and wholeness. It is sided by Strength to show the physical side of well-being, and the Sun, which depicts the emotional well-being that affects and is affected by full health.

As an accessory for this spell, try to obtain a full-length mirror, and have it set up in a well-lit room (sunlit, if possible). Have a place where the cards can be laid out nearby. If you wish to use other accessories, include flowers, candles, crystals and gemstones, and cloth to lay the cards upon. These can be red or orange to symbolize energy and vitality, green to emphasize youth, growth, and healing, or white to represent pure energy and all elements in harmony.

This spell can be performed at anytime, but is best performed early in the morning, especially before an exercise session. This spell will help you start your morning in a good frame of mind and will put your mind in focus for living healthy all day.

To perform this spell, you may use the ritual provided in chapter 1, improvise a ritual of your own, or just proceed by laying out the cards and doing the following meditation, visualization, and affirmation.

Meditation and Visualization

When ready, lay the cards in place in the following order:

* Set your Significator in place while thinking about your desire to remake yourself in a healthier and more perfect form.

* Set the Magician over your Significator while considering some of the steps you will take to bring about these changes: exercise, nutrition, etc.

* Put the World in its place, as indicated on the diagram. Consider all of the areas of your life that will be affected by a holistic well-being with mind and body in harmony.

* To the left of the World, set Strength, while thinking about the strength, vigor, and stamina that you hope to attain and maintain. Visualize yourself utilizing the strength you have to the best possible extent.

* To the right of the World set the Sun in place, as indicated on the diagram, while picturing yourself walking in the sunlight, enjoying the glow of total health.

Once all of the cards are in place, stand in front of the full-length mirror. (If you do not have such a mirror, a smaller mirror will do, or you can just do without.) Study your body while you spread your arms upward and outward. Visualize yourself as a tree, with limbs reaching up to heaven, leaves drawing sustenance from the Sun, roots drawing sustenance from the Earth. Imagine how it would feel to draw the power of the Sun and the Earth and all living things through your body. You feel this energy being processed to build strength, vitality, and wholeness. You feel the power flowing in through your body and out again, making the body stronger and better and very well toned.

As you continue to imagine how this power would flow, look again at yourself in the mirror and see yourself not as you are, but as your ideal self is, as you should be and as you shall be: toned muscles, glowing skin, the radiance of health and beauty.

After you have sustained the visualization exercise in front of the mirror for a few minutes, carefully, and with as much feeling as you can, recite the following affirmation.

Affirmation

"I call upon the strength of the Earth,

the vitality of the Sun,

and the life force within me!

Power flows through my body.

It purges and purifies all that is harmful.

It imbues every cell of my body with radiant health.

Strength and beauty shine through me.

I honor my body.

I shape my body.

I nourish my body with good food and good thoughts.

My mind and body are in harmony,

and I am whole and healthy!

So it is, and so shall it be!"

You may consider the spell closed at this point, or you may close the spell as suggested in chapter 1, or as desired.

Significator

50. To aid healing of physical problems.

*T*his spell surrounds the subject with the qualities needed to restore physical health after such problems as illness, injury, etc. While the previous spell was a general spell to improve and maintain health, this spell is for persons who suffer from some debilitating ailment, and therefore need to focus on defeating that particular problem. Naturally, this spell should not be used in lieu of professional medical treatment. Rather, this spell can supplement professional care, bringing the patient's unconscious mind into harmony with the physical self to facilitate the healing process.

Note: For the healing of health problems that seem to stem more from emotional rather than physical causes, refer to the section on "Emotions."

In this layout, healing qualities flow into the subject. Strength signifies that the individual will have the energy and endurance needed. The Star bestows aid from many sources: the individual's own inner healing potential, spiritual agencies, and other persons such as doctors, nurses, friends, etc., who are needed for professional care and emotional support. The World shows the individual recovered and in full health. The Three of Cups shows celebration of healing and recovery (one of Waite's explanations of the Three of Cups is "a healing to come").

For this spell, have prepared a basin of water and a sponge. (If you want to be fancy, you can use a large silver bowl as your basin.)

If you are performing this spell for someone other than yourself, obtain a doll with a general likeness to that person, and attach something belonging to that person to the doll. Bathe the doll and change the visualizations and affirmations accordingly.

If you wish to use other accessories for this spell, include flowers, as they bespeak vitality and a traditional "get well" message. You can also use candles, crystals and gemstones, and cloth to lay the cards upon. These can be red or orange to confer energy and vitality (and the strength needed to come through an operation), green to emphasize youth, growth, healing and regeneration, or white to represent pure energy and all elements in harmony.

This spell is best performed before going to bed; this will give your unconscious mind a start on accelerating the healing process while you sleep.

You are to perform this spell in the nude. When ready, you may use the ritual provided in chapter 1, improvise a ritual of your own, or just proceed by laying out the cards and doing the following meditation, visualization, and affirmation.

Meditation and Visualization

Lay the cards in place in the following order:

* Set your Significator in place while thinking about your desire to heal the ailment you have been suffering from.

* Set Strength in place, picturing yourself having the strength of health you need, whether it be applied to getting through an operation, fighting an infection, or rebuilding damaged cells.

* Set the Star in place with the reassurance that all healing agencies will be there to help you, whether they be doctors and nurses or ministering angels and spirits.

* Lay down the World, knowing that through this spell you are setting your body and mind in harmony with the life spirit of the Earth and of the universe. You know that the life force will revitalize and regenerate your every cell. Visualize the life force pulsing especially strong in the area or areas of your body that need healing.

* Set the Three of Cups in place and picture yourself living a full and active life following a complete recovery.

After all the cards have been set in place, stand over the basin of water. Close your eyes and imagine that you are floating in a field of stars. The light of the stars shines around you and through you. You reach your hands out, and the magical power of the stars flows into you through your fingertips. Open your eyes and spread your palms out over the water basin. Direct the magical starlight out through your palms, imbuing the water with special power to purify and heal.

Now, take the sponge and wash yourself all over, giving extra attention to any individual parts of your body that need healing. Feel the magically charged water making your body tingle, permeating every cell as you wash yourself.

If your problem is one for which repair and rebuilding of tissues or systems is required, concentrate on how the water is nourishing you. If the problem is disease, envision the water washing away the infection. If your problem is one where systems, hormones, etc., are out of kilter, envision the water relaxing everything and setting every thing in balance, everything right.

After you have completed your sponge bath, carefully, and with as much feeling as possible, say the following affirmation.

Affirmation

"With this spell, I have bathed myself in starlight.

Vitality and power flow through me.

Healing works in me,

coming through many channels,

from many sources.

I am strengthened and purified

within and without.

Every cell of my body is revitalized

by the force that courses through me.

I release all sickness.

I release all pain.

My problem (name it) flows away from me

like a river.

The thing which caused my ailment (name)

is carried away, and is no more.

Whether it be a physical thing,

or a pattern in my thoughts or behavior,

I release it,

and it is carried away by the river of life

that flows through me.

All is now made well.

I am in full health.

I rejoin the dance of life

and I enjoy my wonderful and perfect body!"

You may consider the spell closed at this point, or you may close the spell as suggested in chapter 1, or as desired.

If time permits, perform this spell every day until you have been fully cured of your ailment. If trying to perform this every day should present a problem, then just say the affirmation in the morning when rising, and in the evening before retiring. Know that as time continues, the white light which pervades the universe will continue to flow through your body, purifying, strengthening, and healing you more and ever more.

Houses and Homes

51. For help in finding your dream house.

*P*erform this spell if you want a little extra help in finding the house that will be "just right" for you and your family.

This square, four-card layout suggests the foundations of a home. It suggests a shelter that's firm, well built, and permanent.

The Hermit represents the process of searching. He holds his lamp up to the Four of Wands, which represents a house that is an ideal home and a haven of refuge. Above this is the Six of Cups, the card of sentiment that is used here because you want a home that evokes the happiest memories of your own childhood (or your childhood ideal). The "dream house" is an ideal fabricated from your good memories and ideas of what a perfect home should be. (The graphics of this card also show a beautiful and happy home.) The square is completed by the Ten of Pentacles. This card shows a family enjoying the security of their home, a place where many generations can come together. *Note:* You could substitute the Ten of Cups for the Ten of Pentacles, if you prefer. The Ten of Cups emphasizes the emotional well being the family enjoys in their home, while the Ten of Pentacles emphasizes material well-being.

In advance of performing this spell you will need to get a little "sympathetic" magic started by working on a project that symbolizes the essence of your desire to find the perfect home. It should be a project you can do with your hands, because the establishment of a home requires the devotion and labor of your hands. How much time you have available will determine how big your project will be. Ideas to consider for your project include decorating a doll house or making a model of a house, making a scrapbook with clippings from magazines which show the interiors and exteriors of ideal homes, designing blueprints for houses, making a major improvement (if you already own a home) in order to command a higher selling price, or working on some hope-chest-type item that you want to display once you have a home of your own. When you are ready to perform the spell, have your project nearby, if possible.

As other accessories, you may use candles, flowers, crystals and gemstones, and cloth to lay the cards upon, in shades or combinations of shades of brown, to represent security and rootedness, green for comfort, or white, which is the harmonious blend of all colors, symbolizing all the elements you want to bring together in your ideal home.

To perform this spell, you may combine it with the ritual provided in chapter 1, improvise a ritual of your own, or simply proceed by laying out the cards and doing the following meditation, visualization, and affirmation.

Meditation and Visualization

When ready, set the Hermit in place. Envision yourself going through the house-hunting process, traveling around, looking at homes of all sorts, and considering which type will be just right for you.

Next, lay down the Four of Wands. Visualize yourself having found that dream house, a house with everything you want in a home. Think of feeling elated, because you are able to get that home at a bargain price.

Now, lay down the Six of Cups and think of the happy memories that you are going to make in this home. Think of the celebrations, the warm get-togethers, the good times your family will have, and the lasting memories that will be engendered.

Finally, set the Ten of Pentacles (or Ten of Cups) in place. Think of the comfort and security that your house will give you, your family, and your heirs as the years go by.

After you have finished meditating on the cards and visualizations, carefully, and with as much feeling as you can, recite the following affirmation. (If your dream house project is a portable one that you have been able to set up near the card layout, spread your hands over it while you read the affirmation.)

Affirmation

"As I set these patterns of cards
I create patterns of magic.
I call to me a home, a special home,
the house of my dreams.
Channels are open for me.
My ideal house is made ready for me.
I find it easily.
I find it at a bargain price.
I am prepared to make many happy memories in this home.

I am ready to enjoy many good times in this home.

I make this home a haven of comfort,

serenity, security, and joy

for many years to come.

As I will, so it is

and so shall it be!"

You may consider the spell closed at this point, or you may close it as suggested in the ritual in chapter 1, or as desired.

52. For the successful sale of a house.

*T*his is a spell to attract a buyer to your house, so that you will make a good sale and be financially well-off as a result.

This layout features two 'Four' cards; Fours stand for material foundations and enclosures, and therefore also for house and home. *Note:* In the Waite-Smith deck, the Four of Wands features a castle in the background and is described as 'a haven of refuge.' Also, the man in the Four of Pentacles doesn't have as stern a look.) It is followed by the Six of Pentacles, which is used here to represent your buyer. The man giving out money in this picture is the buyer whom the spell will summon to your house. The Four of Pentacles shows the outcome. This card represents you as content and considerably enriched as a result of having made a good sale, and already in possession of your next home (if that is what you desire).

As necessary accessories for this spell, include six coins that you will bless during the affirmation. (After performing the spell, you will bury one coin at each corner of your property, one at the beginning of your walkway, and one under or near your front door or threshold.) Also, if you have already placed an ad for your house in a newspaper, have the ad clipped out and on hand for the spell. If you wish to use other accessories, use candles, flowers, crystals and gemstones, and cloth to lay the cards upon, in shades or combinations of shades of gold to create attraction and wealth coming in, and green for money, security, and prosperity.

To perform this spell, you may combine it with the ritual provided in chapter 1, improvise a ritual of your own, or simply proceed by laying out the cards and doing the following meditation, visualization, and affirmation.

Meditation and Visualization

When ready, set the Four of Wands in place. Think of the things you've done to make this house desirable to a buyer. Think of all of the good features that your house has to offer. If you have the ad clipping, hold it and read it for a moment, then set it underneath this card.

Now, set the Six of Pentacles in place. Envision a shadowy figure, perhaps just a vague silhouette of a person driving up to your house, coming up your walkway, coming into your house and being totally overcome with the knowledge that this house will be perfect for his or her needs and the needs of his or her family. This person has the money all ready, and is willing to pay you a good price. Take up the six coins you have ready. Hold them in your hands while you continue this visualization, then set them down on top of the Six of Pentacles.

Finally, set the Four of Pentacles in place. Picture yourself being content and happy because you have made a good sale. Consider what you want to do with the money from the sale of your house. If you desire a new house, think about the love and care you will lavish on your it.

After you have finished meditating on the cards and visualizations, take up the coins once again and warm them with your hands as you carefully, and with as much feeling as you can, recite the following affirmation.

Affirmation

"As I work this spell
the magical images take life
and call to me the buyers that I desire.
My house is desirable.
Many persons are drawn to this house.
Many persons want to buy this house.
Many good offers are made for this house.

I choose the best offer.
I am happy and enriched,
and the purchaser is happy.
As I will, so it is
and so shall it be!"

You may consider the spell closed at this point, or you may close it as suggested in the ritual in chapter 1, or as desired. Once the spell is closed, bury one coin at each corner of your property, one at the beginning of your walkway, and one under or near your front door or threshold. Let the coins remain there after you have sold the house, for they now belong to the spirits of the land, and will continue to attract prosperity for the next inhabitants.

Jobs and Job Hunting

53. To win a job.

*P*erform this spell if you have your heart set on winning a certain job. The layout in the form of descending stairs shows the job coming down to you, and the responsibilities you seek being handed down to you. The first card is the Emperor, which can represent the company or institution that you want to work for, or a specific person, such as a boss or personnel officer, who has the power to hire you. (If you know that the person in charge of hiring is a woman or if the company or institution has a feminine "spirit" or "feel" to it, substitute the Empress.) Judgement, the middle card, signifies that the employer judges you to be the best candidate; it also signifies employment and the changes and upgrading in your lifestyle that come with the job. The Eight of Pentacles shows you hard at work at your new job, enjoying your work and being totally absorbed in what you are doing. *Note:* If you can find images in one of your Tarot cards that more clearly suggest the type of work you have in mind, you can substitute that card for the Eight of Pentacles.

In advance of performing this spell, go to the building where you would like to work and, if possible, walk around its perimeter. (If you are sure that's where you want to work, even if you haven't had an interview, you could do this at the time you drop by to pick up an application or submit your résumé; otherwise do this after your first interview, or whenever you have made up your mind that that is the job you want.) Start on the east side of the building, and proceed south, west, north, and then back to where you started. If something prevents you from walking around the building itself, then walk around the block that it is situated on. (If geographical features completely prevent you from encircling the area, don't worry—you can still perform the rest of the spell.)

While you are taking your walk, if you can do so inconspicuously, collect some material, such as leaves or a handful of dirt or dust, from each of the four sides of the building, as well as from near the front entrance or walkway where employees come and go. Take these things home and put them in a little bag or pouch along with some strands or clippings of your own hair. By mingling these elements, you will create an affinity and open a channel for sympathetic magic. Have this pouch on hand when you perform the spell, and, if possible, carry it in your pocket, purse, or briefcase when you go in for interviews.

As additional accessories for this spell, include near your card layout your résumé or application, objects that symbolize or are used in the job you intend to perform, as well as materials from the company you want to work for, such as its want ad, publicity brochures, annual reports, etc. If you wish to use other accessories, use candles, flowers, crystals and gemstones, and cloth to lay the cards upon, in shades or combinations of shades of gold or silver for attraction and prosperity, or white to represent pure psychic energy.

Perform this spell as soon as possible once you've decided which job you would like to have.

To perform this spell, you may combine it with the ritual provided in chapter 1, improvise a ritual of your own, or simply proceed by laying out the cards and doing the following meditation, visualization, and affirmation.

Meditation and Visualization

When ready, set the Emperor in place. Think of the company that you want to work for and any bosses and personnel officers that you have already met. Hold an image of them in your mind for a moment. Visualize yourself sending them good energy in the form of white light, in order to open a channel of good feeling between you.

Next, set Judgement in place. Envision the desired employer making a decision in your favor and contacting you. Picture yourself being notified that the job is yours. Think of the elation that you will feel upon getting employment and being able to change and upgrade your lifestyle as a result.

Finally, set the Eight of Pentacles in place. Envision yourself settling in to your new job in your new work surroundings. Think of the fulfillment you will find in doing a job that's exactly right for you.

After you have finished meditating on the cards and visualizations, take up the pouch of materials you were able to collect from the company grounds. If you were unable to assemble those materials, take up any materials you do have that symbolize the job you want to win. Warm them with your hands as you carefully recite the following affirmation.

Affirmation

"With these cards and with this spell,

I craft magical images.

These images serve as a template

for that which I desire.

(Name of company or person in charge of hiring)

sees that my qualifications are good.

(Name) knows that I will be an asset to the company.

I am the one (name) wants.

Good news comes to me,

the job is mine!

I enjoy the job.

I do well at my job.

My job rewards me and fulfills me.

As I will, so it is

and so shall it be!"

You may consider the spell closed at this point, or you may close it as suggested in the ritual in chapter 1, or as desired.

54. To gain a job interview with a potential employer.

*P*erform this spell if you've put in applications or sent résumés to a number of potential employers that look promising. You may not yet know which one you'd like to work for—but you would like to get interviews so you'll know your options.

In this layout, the Eight of Pentacles symbolizes your desire to work in a certain field (if you can find a Tarot card that more clearly suggests the type of work you want to do, you can substitute that card for the Eight of Pentacles). The Emperor represents the companies or institutions that you've applied to, as well as the individual persons who will have the power to hire you. The Page of Wands is used here to represent a call to come in for an interview, as one of its traditional meanings is that of messages pertaining to employment.

As accessories for this spell, have materials pertaining to your job hunt, such as want ads, copies of cover letters, applications, résumés, etc., near your card layout. You can also include objects that symbolize or are used in the job you intend to perform as accessories to have on hand. If you wish to use other accessories, use candles, flowers, crystals and gemstones, and cloth to lay the cards upon, in shades or combinations of shades of gold or silver for attraction and prosperity, or white to represent pure psychic energy.

Perform this spell once you've begun the process of submitting résumés and applications. To perform this spell, you may combine it with the ritual provided in chapter 1, improvise a ritual of your own, or simply proceed by laying out the cards and doing the following meditation, visualization, and affirmation.

Meditation and Visualization

When ready, set the Eight of Pentacles in place. Think about the line of work you intend to get into and the actions you have been taking to look for a job. Set down the Emperor while visualizing generalized images of the types of companies you'd like to work for. Go over the names of the specific companies that have received or are about to receive your applications.

Finally, set the Page of Wands in place while visualizing yourself being swamped with phone calls and letters requesting interviews, giving you all the options and opportunities you want.

After you have finished meditating on the cards and visualizations, take up any accessories you have that pertain to your job hunt while warming them with your hands as you carefully, and with as much feeling as you can, recite the following affirmation.

Affirmation

"As I set forth these patterns of cards
I create patterns of magic.
Magic channels are open for me.
I have made myself known
to those from whom I seek interviews.
Many calls and many letters come to me.
I have many invitations
to many interviews.
I look forward to all the opportunities
that are here for me.
As I will, so it is
and so shall it be!"

You may consider the spell closed at this point, or you may close it as suggested in the ritual in chapter 1, or as desired.

55. To gain a promotion or a raise.

*T*his layout takes the form of an ascending staircase, symbolizing job advancement and the betterment of your condition. The Emperor represents the person who is empowered to give you the raise or the promotion you desire. (If that person is a woman, use the Empress.) Judgement represents the change in condition which you desire, change which brings rewards for your achievements and an awakening to new possibilities. The Three of Pentacles is the culminating card, showing you at work while implying status, honor, advancement, and improvement of your work conditions. This spell also evokes one of the older interpretations of this card, which is "forces taken from the occult to obtain realisations in the physical world." (Grimaud 42). If there is a Tarot card, however, that better symbolizes the reward or elevation you seek, use that in place of the Three of Pentacles.

Prior to performing this spell, write out a list of your accomplishments, as well as the rewards you desire and deserve. This list will be used to lay the cards out upon. If you wish to use other accessories, use candles, flowers, crystals and gemstones, and cloth to lay everything out upon, in shades or combinations of shades of gold for expansiveness, liberality, and prosperity; green for growth, opportunity, money, and ambition, or white to represent pure psychic energy.

To work this spell, you may combine it with the ritual provided in chapter 1, improvise a ritual of your own, or proceed by laying out the cards and doing the following meditation, visualization, and affirmation.

Meditation and Visualization

When ready, set the Emperor in place on top of your list of accomplishments and desires. For a moment, hold in your mind the image of the company or individual that has the power to promote you or give you a raise.

Next, set Judgement in place as indicated in the diagram. As you contemplate your expected good news, personal transformation, and elevation to higher things, think of the elation you will feel upon learning of your advancement.

Finally, set the Three of Pentacles in place. Visualize yourself at work, facing new challenges and enjoying the honors that have been bestowed upon you.

After you have finished meditating on the cards and visualizations, carefully, and with as much feeling as you can, recite the following affirmation.

Affirmation

"I call upon these magical images
to give life to my desires!
(Name of employer) recognizes my worth.
The good news comes to me:
The promotion (or raise) that I want is mine!
Recognition is mine.
Honor is mine.
Advancement is mine.
Financial rewards and increases are mine.

I am ready to enjoy the changes and challenges
my new position brings me.
As I will, so it is
and so shall it be!"

You may consider the spell closed at this point, or you may close it as suggested in the ritual in chapter 1, or as desired.

When finished with this spell, fold up the list you made, take it to work, and keep it there in a secret place.

Knowledge

56. To tap the subconscious mind for knowledge.

We all possess untapped resources in our unconscious minds. This spell will help bring you more in tune with the knowledge and guidance that is to be found within you. It can be performed as a general-purpose spell to make an initial contact with your unconscious mind, enabling you to better hear the inner voice. It can also be performed as a special purpose spell, used when there is a specific question you want answered.

This crown-shaped layout recalls the ancient occult symbolism which likens knowledge to a crown of glory (it also acknowledges the associations between head and mind). The first card is the Moon, which is the card symbolizing the depths of the unconscious mind. The High Priestess is the receptacle of knowledge; in combination with the Moon, she represents your desire and innate ability to probe and study the hidden wisdom taken from your subconscious. The Hermit represents your desire to bring this knowledge to light.

As a necessary accessory for this spell, have near your layout a simple candle, one that you can concentrate on without distraction. Do not light it until instructed to do so.

If you wish to use other accessories for this spell, use additional candles, flowers, crystals and gemstones, and cloth to lay the cards upon, in shades or combinations of shades of blue, the color of introspection; purple, which symbolizes psychic knowledge and understanding; green, which the Druids regarded as the color of knowledge; or black and white, which symbolize the Kabbalistic pillars of wisdom which you see in some versions of the High Priestess card. (Black represents understanding because it absorbs all light, and white represents the quintessence of Divine Light.)

If you are performing this spell because you need help with a certain line of research or study, lay the cards out on top of a book on the subject you are undertaking.

If this spell is to be used for general purposes, perform it before going to bed. For specific purposes, perform it whenever you feel it's necessary.

To work this spell, you may use the ritual provided in chapter 1, improvise a ritual of your own, or just proceed by laying out the cards and doing the following meditation, visualization, and affirmation.

Meditation and Visualization

When ready, lay out the cards according to the diagram.

First, set the Moon in place. Study the archetypal images in this card as you consider its association with the seemingly impenetrable depths of the subconscious mind. This is the unknown realm of imagination, mystery, magic, illusions, inspiration, intuition, and dreams.

Next, set the High Priestess in place. Think of your own desire to have access to hidden knowledge, to be able to unlock any mystery.

Finally, set the Hermit in place. Picture yourself holding up a lantern which sheds light all around you, with the knowledge that this light will illumine the secrets you want to uncover. Know that everything will be brought out of the darkness and made clear to you as the light penetrates all illusions and self-deceptions.

After you have completed the meditations, take the special candle that until now has remained unlit. Light it while saying:

> "The image of this flame
>
> is the key to my unconscious mind.
>
> Whenever I call upon this image,
>
> hidden knowledge is brought to light."

Stare at the candle flame until its image has been burned into your mind. Then, close your eyes and hold the image of the candle in your mind for as long as you possibly can.

When you feel that the image of the candle flame has been indelibly etched into your memory, carefully recite the following affirmation.

Affirmation

"I look deep within me.
I draw wisdom from the depths
of my unconscious mind.
All knowledge is here for me.
All channels of guidance are open for me.
Everything I want to know is revealed to me.
Everything is made clear to me.
As I will, so it is
and so shall it be."

You may put the candle or candles out and close the spell at this point, or you may close the spell as suggested in the rite in chapter 1, or as desired.

If this spell has been performed for general purposes, be sure to keep a diary near your bed, so that you can record any interesting dreams you've had as a result of doing this spell. (It's a good idea to continue to record your dreams each night after working this spell.)

With the suggestion that you have put into your subconscious as a result of having performed this ceremony, you now have a hypnotic key to utilize anytime you seek specific information.

Whenever you need to call on your unconscious for something—say if you seek intuitive information, have a mental block, have forgotten something, etc.—sit down, submit the question to your mind by stating it out loud, relax, call the image of the flame to your memory, and concentrate on it for a few moments. If the information you seek does not come into your mind immediately after doing this, just put your question out of your mind and follow your first impulse, even if it's to do something silly or seemingly irrelevant like playing a video game, doing some housecleaning, or whatever. You'll be surprised to find that often the information will pop into your mind later, when you least expect it.

Legal Undertakings

57. For success in a legal undertaking.

*T*his is a general-purpose spell to ensure favorable outcomes for legal matters. This layout symbolizes favorable judgements being handed down. Justice applies to the legal establishment and the making of decisions that are necessary to dispense justice and maintain law and order. The Eight of Wands represents swiftness in approaching goals, to help prevent you from being inconvenienced by the slowness of the legal system and all the bureaucracies involved. Judgement is here applied literally for a favorable judgement. Since legal proceedings always involve paperwork, you probably have lots of papers pertaining to your matter. Stack them in a pile, and when you do the spell, you can lay the cards out on top of them. If you wish to use other accessories for this spell, use candles, flowers, crystals and gemstones, and cloth to lay the cards upon, in shades or combinations of shades of white, representing purity of intentions, or purple, which stands for dignity and authority, and is also the color worn by American law faculties. If financial gain is the hoped-for outcome of your legal action, consider including shades of green and gold.

Perform this spell just before or soon after beginning or becoming involved in a legal action.

To work this spell, you may use the ritual provided in chapter 1, improvise a ritual of your own, or just proceed by laying out the cards and doing the following meditation, visualization, and affirmation.

Meditation and Visualization

When ready, lay out the cards according to the diagram.

First, set Justice in place (set it on top of your legal papers, if you have them). Envision everyone involved in your action—lawyers, judges, witnesses, etc.—as being friendly, benevolent, and favorably disposed toward you. Picture the legal authorities considering your case, weighing all the merits of your argument; picture them smiling as they agree that you should win your case.

Next, set the Eight of Wands in place. Picture your case being handled efficiently. There are no barriers or delays; the legal machinery moves smoothly, steadily, and swiftly as all the necessary actions are taken to conclude your case.

Finally, set Judgement in place. Picture your elation as the judgement is announced— you have won your case! Think of the favorable impact and the positive changes you will be able to make, now that Justice has ruled in your favor.

When you have finished your meditation, spread your hands over the card layout, and carefully recite the following affirmation.

Affirmation

"With these cards and with this spell,

I call upon all good forces

to help me win my case!

Justice is done.

The court hears me,

the court favors me.

All moves swiftly.

All moves easily.

A decision is made,

victory is mine!

My case is won,

and harmony and balance

are restored.

So it is,

and so shall it be!"

You may close the spell at this point, or you may close the spell as suggested in the rite in chapter 1, or as desired.

Note: When you have to make court appearances, you can carry the Justice card in your purse or pocket to serve as a good luck amulet.

Love and Romance

58. To attract love.

*P*erform this spell if you have been yearning for a great love to enter your life. This spell calls upon arcane forces to bring the ideal man or woman to you.

The first card in this layout is the Star, showing powerful, unseen, and fateful forces opening channels to bring your ideal lover to you. The Knight of Cups represents a person who brings love into your life, who involves you in an affair—the proverbial "knight in shining armor." According to some Tarot experts, the knight can represent either a male or a female. However, if you're calling for an ideal woman and are uncomfortable with the Knight, then substitute the High Priestess, the Empress, or one of the Queens. In fact, if you have a very strong idea of what you want your ideal man or woman to be, put any card you feel best represents your ideal mate in this position. (Refer to appendix 1, "Choosing a Significator.") The Lovers here uses its literal meaning.

As accessories for this spell, obtain thirteen red candles (do not light these candles until instructed to, later in the spell). If you wish to use other accessories, include additional candles, flowers, crystals and gemstones, and cloth to lay the cards upon, in shades of red, the color of human love, or white, representing pure psychic energy.

Perform this spell at night before going to bed.

To work this spell, you may use the ritual provided in chapter 1, improvise a ritual of your own, or just proceed by laying out the cards and doing the following meditation, visualization, and affirmation.

Meditation and Visualization

When ready, lay out the cards according to the diagram. First, set the Star in place. After you have done so, spread out your arms and say:

> "I call upon all good spirits!
> I call upon all karmic forces!
> I call upon the wide-ruling powers!
> Make smooth the way,
> that my love may be brought to me!"

Think about your desire to enlist occult forces in helping you to find a true love, a soul mate.

Next, set down the Knight of Cups (or whichever card you have chosen to put in this position). Think about what you want in the ideal man or woman.

Finally, set the Lovers in place. Spend some time daydreaming about the sort of romantic adventures you would like to have.

When your visualizations are complete, take the thirteen red candles, and use them to make a circle around your card layout. Light each candle, and then, with as much feeling as you can, recite the following affirmation.

Affirmation

"I call for love, and love comes to me
guided by the light of my flames.
Whether it be from near
or from far,
My love is drawn to me.
I give love,
I receive love.
Our love is passionate,
our love is intense as flame.
Our love is long and lasting.
As I desire, so I have love,
and so shall it be!"

You may close the spell at this point by putting out the candles and putting away the cards, or you may close the spell as suggested in the rite in chapter 1, or as desired.

<table>
<tr>
<td>**Your Significator**</td>
<td>
The Lovers</td>
<td>**Other Person's Significator**</td>
</tr>
</table>

59. To win the love of a certain person.

*P*erform this spell when you desire to awaken love in a special person. The meaning of these cards and this layout is fairly obvious: your Significator and the Significator of your object of desire are brought together as lovers. (To choose Significators, refer to appendix 1.)

As accessories for this spell, obtain thirteen red candles; do not light these candles until instructed to, later in the spell. Also, if you can obtain a photo or any personal belongings, or anything that has made contact with the person you are infatuated with, include these to lend focus to the spell. If you wish to use other accessories, include additional candles, flowers, crystals and gemstones, and cloth to lay the cards upon in shades of red, the color of human love, or white, representing pure psychic energy.

Perform this spell at night before going to bed.

To work this spell, you may use the ritual provided in chapter 1, improvise a ritual of your own, or just proceed by laying out the cards and doing the following meditation, visualization, and affirmation.

Meditation and Visualization

When ready, lay out the cards according to the diagram.

First, set your loved one's Significator in place. If you have a photo or something that belongs to or has touched that person, take it up at this time, and warm it with your hands. Say that person's name aloud three times, and try to hold his or her image in your mind for the space of nine heartbeats.

Next, set your Significator in place, leaving a space so that you will have room to set the next card between the two Significators. *Note:* If possible, try to have the two Significators facing each other. This means that it may be necessary to have your Significator on the right, and the other Significator on the left, even though this is different from what you see in the diagram. For a few moments, concentrate on your own desire for the other person.

Finally, set the Lovers in place. Spend some time daydreaming about the sort of romantic adventures you would like to have with the special person you have in mind.

When your visualizations are complete, use the thirteen red candles to make a circle around your card layout. Light each candle, and then, with as much feeling as you can, recite the following affirmation.

Affirmation

"With these cards and with this spell,

these images take on life

and give life to my desires.

I call for (name of beloved), and (name)

comes to me, guided by the light of my flames.

Whether it be from near

or from far,

(name) is drawn to me.

I give love to (name),

I receive love from (name).

Our love is passionate,

our love is intense as flame.

Our love is long and lasting.

As I desire, so do we love,

and so shall it be!"

You may close the spell at this point by putting out the candles and putting away the cards, or you may close the spell as suggested in the rite in chapter 1, or as desired.

A caution regarding love spells: Spells that try to win the love of another person are among the most problematic of all spells, but I include this one because it is also among the most in demand by readers. I believe that for attraction to take place and a relationship to be successful, there should be a certain chemistry between the two individuals, as well as maturity, mutual respect, and the ability to handle commitment. Consequently, if you feel the need to do a love spell on someone, that person is probably wrong for you. Indeed, I question whether any love spell can long hold up against the resistant forces it will encounter if the two individuals are wrong for each other—especially if the spell caster has unethical motives, such as trying to break up someone's marriage. The exceptions would be cases where you are trying to kindle an existing love that has cooled off a bit, where you're trying to encourage the spark of love in someone who is too distracted or too shy to approach you, or where you are a member of an ethnic group with a tradition of arranged marriages, and are trying to promote the growth of affection within such a relationship.

Luck

The Star

Significator

21 The World 21

60. To attract good luck.

*T*his spell helps to "set things up" around you. It adjusts the flow of events so that things start happening in your favor, and the world begins being a better place for you to live in. In doing this spell, you give a beneficient "push" to circumstance.

This layout shows spiritual powers descending to create a state of good luck. The Star represents forces beyond human control, help from diverse sources, and great good fortune. The Significator card representing you is superimposed over the Wheel of Fortune to show that you have the advantage of the forces of change. The Wheel represents changing circumstances and is associated with Fortuna, the ancient Roman goddess who bestowed good luck on those she favored. The World is the card that symbolizes a perfect life. In using this spell, you are reaching up into a higher plane of existence, up into Plato's "highest ideal," and pulling it down through *you* into the solid manifestation of the World. It is, in short, the world as it should be and as you in doing this spell desire it to be.

For this spell, you may select some special object, which can be charged with power in the course of the spell, to be used as a good luck charm. It is not actually necessary to select a good luck charm; the performing of the spell itself will bring you lasting luck. (If you do wish to have a charm, think of it as a nice little "extra"; however, do not feel that you have to be dependent on it. Your luck will not be affected if you lose the charm or do not have it always near you.) You may choose a traditional good luck symbol, such as a horseshoe, rabbit's foot, four-leaf clover, etc., or you may prefer some personal object such as a piece of jewelry, or any other object that has a good feel to you. Any one of the cards in this layout would also make a suitable good luck charm.

If you wish to use other accessories for this spell, use candles, flowers, precious metals, crystals, and gemstones, in tones of gold and silver. Gold symbolizes wealth and expansiveness, and silver stands for purity of understanding and the state of being at harmony with all . . . so that "all" is in harmony with you. The combination of gold and silver also shows both the solar and lunar forces of nature working in your favor.

To perform this spell, you may use the ritual provided in chapter 1, improvise a ritual of your own, or just proceed by laying out the cards and doing the following meditation, visualization, and affirmation.

Meditation and Visualization

When ready, put the Star in place. Visualize that you are floating in a sea of shining stars. Their light shines through you and their power magnetizes you so that all the good forces of the world are gathered about you and clothe you in the brilliant raiment of success and good fortune. The power called down from the stars themselves courses through your spirit and soul. Close your eyes for a few moments and feel, as clearly as you can, just how this would feel. Savor the sensation.

Next, set down the Wheel of Fortune and then set your Significator on top of it. Note that your card is at the balance-point of the layout: you are the natural nexus-point for all of the forces that are called forth, and you're going to be the one who benefits. Close your eyes again for a few minutes and picture yourself at the whirling center of vast tides of glowing, beautiful light. They course over you, and through you, and swirl about you. You become stronger and better and just plain lucky!

Finally, add the World to the layout. Image as clear as you can that, like the figure on the card, you are at the center and the balance-point of all forces and events of humankind, of the sky, and of the Earth. The green wreath is here, the elemental Earth herself, drawing in the vast powers of light you have called forth, and pulsing them back through you. Again, *you* are at the center of it all, and benefiting enormously by it. Close your eyes for a moment and feel the sensation of the good powers that go through your being into the Earth, and back through you again.

At this point, it will greatly enhance the power of this spell if you emulate the figure in the World by doing your own interpretive dance-of-life. If your space is too restrictive or you feel uncomfortable about dancing, just make wavy motions over the card layout with your hands. Imagine that you are using your hands to manipulate cosmic energies and weave the threads of a good fate.

If you have selected some object that you would like to have for a good luck charm, direct your attention to the object at this time. Rub the object between your hands and feel energy surging through your body and flowing out through your hands, imbuing the object with power.

When you feel that you have expended enough energy on the above-mentioned actions, recite the following affirmation.

Affirmation

"I draw power from the stars

and send them, through me, into the Earth,

then back through myself once again.

Fortune and luck are with me,

surrounding all that I do

and following me everywhere.

All who are about me prosper,

as do I.

And I become better, stronger, and

more lucky than ever before.

By all the high and mystical powers

through whom Fortune shines,

So shall it be!"

You may consider the spell closed at this point, or you may close the spell as suggested in the rite in chapter 1, or as desired.

Wheel of Fortune

Significator

The Star

61. For good luck in games or gambling.

*T*his spell helps you to achieve a winning attitude to boost your luck, stepping up your innate talents to get you "on a roll." A positive outlook will turn fortune in your direction. It adjusts the flow of chance so that things start happening in your favor, and circumstance just happens to incline your way while you keep this very positive mindset.

This layout shows cosmic powers being directed toward a very specific goal. The Star represents forces beyond human control, help from diverse sources, and great good fortune. In using this card in a magical spell you are reaching into the universe's vast reservoir of "good vibes" and marvelous happenstance, and pulling it up through *you* (represented by the Significator card) to press your own desire upon the Wheel of Fortune. Here the verbal connotations and graphic symbolism of the Wheel are applied to games of chance, so those things begin going your way every time that you play! By the way, the Wheel is the ancient symbol of the goddess Fortuna, patroness of gamblers and giver of luck.

For this spell, you may select some special object that can be charged with power in the course of the spell to be used as a good luck charm. It is not truly necessary to select a good-luck charm; the performing of the spell itself will create a winning outlook. (If you do wish to have a charm, think of it as a nice little "extra"; however, do not feel that you have to be dependent on it. Your luck will not be affected if you lose the charm or do not have it always near you.) You may choose a traditional good luck symbol or something that more specifically symbolizes good luck in gaming, such as a special coin. You may prefer some personal object such as a piece of jewelry, or any other object that has a good feel to you. (Any one of the cards in this layout could also make a suitable good luck charm.)

If you wish to use other accessories for this spell, use candles of gold and coins of silver. Also use gold and silver cloth to lay the cards upon and flowers, crystals and gemstones with tones suggesting the solar and lunar luminaries. Gold symbolizes wealth and expansiveness, of course. Silver stands for a purity of understanding and the state of being at harmony with all—so that "all" is in harmony with you! The combination of gold and silver also shows both the solar and lunar forces of nature working in your favor.

The best time for doing this spell is just before you go out to do some serious gambling. It's important for you to psyche yourself up, and to keep yourself that way. (You might also want to do this one the evening before you hit Las Vegas, or Reno, go out for a lottery ticket, or when you finally decide you want to go out for an evening of bingo!)

To perform this spell, you may use the ritual provided in chapter 1, improvise a ritual of your own, or just proceed by laying out the cards and doing the following meditation, visualization, and affirmation.

Meditation and Visualization

When ready, put the Star in place. Close your eyes and visualize that you are the most charismatic gambler of all time, and that you are standing beneath a sky filled with stars. Image a shining star that appears before you and takes on the shape of a mysterious female figure clothed all in gold. She takes both her hands in yours, and you feel warmth flowing from her hands into yours. You raise up your hands to look at them, and you see that they are shining with a golden glow. The sure feeling of "being hot" is with you; you notice that you are wrapped in a golden glow that gives you the feeling of being unbeatable! Feel within yourself, as clearly as you can, just how this would be. Savor the sensations.

Next, set down the Significator—the card that you have chosen to symbolize yourself. Note that your card is at the balance-point between the other two: you yourself are the natural nexus-point of all of the good luck that comes from the stars themselves, and which *you* will bring into being as you play the games of chance. Continue to visualize yourself with golden hands and bathed in a golden glow.

Finally, add the Wheel as the highest step of your spell. As you put down this card, feel clearly within yourself that you now have the final key to it all, that you now have the "magic touch," and that with this magical ingredient, you will get hot—you'll "stay on a roll" until you've won. Picture yourself spinning the wheel and winning every time. Imagine just what it will be like to *win* and win big! Picture yourself winning at the game or games you intend to play. Picture others congratulating you, and asking how you did it. Feel this exultant sensation, holding the feeling as long as you can.

If you have selected some object that you would like to have for a good luck charm, direct your attention to the object at this time. Rub the object between your hands and feel energy surging through your body and flowing out through your hands, imbuing the object with power so that it too takes on the golden glow.

When you feel that you have spent enough time with the ritual visualizations, recite the following affirmation.

Affirmation

"I call forth the powers of good fortune!

I draw powers from the stars

and weave them into my prosperity.

As I play the games of chance

all the signs are with me . . .

and nothing can stop me . . .

I am a winner, and I win big. [repeat five times]

Fortune smiles upon me

as never before.

By all the high and mystical powers

through whom fortune shines,

So it is, and so shall it be!"

You may consider the spell closed at this point, or you may close the spell as suggested in the rite in chapter 1, or as desired.

A note about winning: I have observed that sometimes the most impressive windfalls happen not to the persons who most desperately need the luck, but rather to those who are lighthearted. It seems that there is a playful force in the universe that blesses happy hearts with serendipity. When you go out to play your games of chance, I urge you to avoid any feelings of desperation—any feelings that you "need" to win. Instead, maintain your "I shall win!" feelings combined with a happy-go-lucky attitude. May the best of fortune go with you!

Money

First Significator

Second Significator

62. To encourage debtors to repay debts.

*T*his is a spell to help you get your money repaid when it's past time, and you've decided to start leaning on the one(s) who owe you. You've done a favor, and now it's time you were paid back!

This layout shows strong forces being summoned to start a flow of money from your debtors back to you. The Ace of Swords represents the forces you invoke to bring pressure to bear on your debtor(s), and the Ace of Pentacles represents the money owed you. The Six of Pentacles signifies the transfer of money from your debtor(s) (First Significator) to you (Second Significator). The Six of Pentacles shows your debtors having the ability to pay you back in full.

If you have decided to try to collect from several debtors at once, use the King of Pentacles in the First Significator position. The King of Pentacles represents someone who is able to give you financial help, so it can be used here as a general card representing the people who need to repay you. If you are trying to collect from just one debtor, choose an appropriate Significator (see appendix 1).

This spell will require burning a special candle each day for nine days, so obtain nine fairly large red candles. Here, red is used to symbolize force and immediate action. Make a list of who owes you money and how much, then inscribe the amounts as well as the names or initials of the debtors on each of the nine special candles. Do not light the special candles until instructed to do so at the appropriate point in the spell. Include these near the card layout. As additional necessary accessories, have a sharp knife and a silver coin on hand.

If you wish to use other accessories, decorate the area with additional candles, flowers, crystals and gemstones, and cloth to lay the cards upon in shades or combinations of shades of red for action, green for money, gold for attraction, or white for pure psychic energy.

Choose a time of the day when you will be undisturbed, and perform this spell at the same time each day for nine days.

To perform this spell, you may use it in combination with the ritual in chapter 1, improvise a ritual of your own, or just proceed by laying out the cards and doing the following meditation, visualization, and affirmation.

Meditation and Visualization

When ready, set your debtor's Significator (first) in place, and immediately set the Ace of Swords on top of it. If you require legal action in collecting your money, add the Justice card, putting it between the first Significator and the Ace of Swords. If you have signatures of your debtors or something belonging to them, take them up at this time, and hold the point of the knife to them. If you do not have such objects, just hold the point of your knife to the Significator card with the Ace of Swords on top of it. Envision your debtor or debtors feeling a sudden compulsion to pay you. They feel like there is a sharp sword prodding them along, and they sense that they'll find no peace until they pay you.

Set the Six of Pentacles in place, as indicated in the diagram. Money will be spread around, and the only way it can be spread is in your direction. Think on it, and fix that idea very strongly in your mind.

Now, set your Significator (second) in place and immediately set the Ace of Pentacles on top of it. Visualize your creditor coming to terms with you, so that the debt is paid in full. Take up the silver coin and warm it with your hands, taking in the feeling of it while you picture yourself holding the full payment in your hands.

After you have spent sufficient time meditating on the cards and visualizations, take one of the special large red candles you have prepared and light it. Then, carefully, and with as much feeling as you can, recite the following affirmation.

Affirmation

"I call upon the fundamental justice
which pervades all things!
I call upon the forces of the universe
that do decree and enforce this justice.
Powerful forces are set in motion,
and my debtors must obey.
Everything that is owed me
is paid in full.
That which is mine is readily handed over.
Money comes to me
and all is made well.
So it is, and so shall it be!"

You may consider the spell closed until the next day, or you may close it as suggested in the ritual in chapter 1, or as desired.

Allow the candle to burn out. Repeat this spell every day until all of the nine candles have been burned down.

Significator

Page of Pentacles

Knight of Pentacles

63. To attract money and prosperity.

*T*his is a spell to open channels to bring money in from many sources, both expected and unexpected. The cards are laid out in a pyramid, with you at the top and supported by many of the factors that make for well-being and prosperity.

The Ace of Pentacles is at the center of the foundation of the pyramid, standing for money coming in, wealth, and success. The Six of Pentacles portrays you so successful that you are able to spread your wealth around. The Ten of Pentacles represents family wealth and inheritances; not only you but also your loved ones will be able to enjoy what you've gained. The Page of Pentacles here represents news of a windfall (the Page could also represent the messenger or the means by which news of wealth arrives). Since Knights represent the coming or going of matters, the Knight of Pentacles here represents new and unexpected sources of money and prosperity. And of course, you are at the top of it all, where you deserve to be! *Note:* If your Significator is normally the Page or Knight of Pentacles, put the Magician at the top.

As accessories for this spell, you will need six small coins that afterwards will be buried or hidden at the four corners of your property or apartment as well as by or under your front door and walkway. If you wish to use other accessories for this spell, decorate the area with silver coins and candles, flowers, crystals and gemstones, and cloth to lay the cards upon in shades or combinations of shades of gold for attraction and wealth, and green for money, growth, and prosperity.

To perform this spell, you may use it in combination with the ritual in chapter 1, improvise a ritual of your own, or just proceed by laying out the cards and doing the following meditation, visualization, and affirmation.

Meditation and Visualization

When ready, set your Significator in place. Meditate on the thought that you have the power to shape the image of what you want—money and prosperity—and send it off into the living universe. Positively affirm your wishes, and your desires are turned into reality.

Next, set the Page of Pentacles in place, as indicated on the diagram. Imagine yourself being notified of a windfall. Try to feel that state of elation that you would experience.

Set the Knight of Pentacles down. Envision money coming in to you from many sources, sources that you may expect, and sources that come as a surprise.

Set the Ace of Pentacles in place, as indicated on the diagram. Continue to visualize money coming in. Picture yourself handling lots of money, flipping through stacks of paper money, running your hands through piles of coins.

Set the Six of Pentacles in place, to the left of the Ace of Pentacles. Contemplate the ways you'd like to spend your money; visualize yourself spreading your money around,

Finally, set the Ten of Pentacles in place. Imagine the sensation of having your family and your friends share in your prosperity and comfort.

After you have finished meditating on the cards and visualizations, take up the six coins that have been set aside for this purpose and warm them in your hands as you carefully, and with as much feeling as you can, recite the following affirmation.

Affirmation

"As I work this spell
these magical images take life.
I call for money
and money comes to me.
Channels of money and abundance
are open to me,
and money comes from many sources.
Money is good for me,
and I do good things with my money.
My money increases.
I thank the living universe
for the good it sends me.
So it is, and so shall it be."

You may consider the spell closed at this point, or you may close it as suggested in the ritual in chapter 1, or as desired.

After you have closed the spell, bury one coin at each corner of your property; if you live in an apartment, you can bury them at the four corners of your building, or slip the coins under the rugs in the corners of your apartment. Also, bury a coin at the beginning of your walkway, and one under or near your front door or threshold; for apartment dwellers, slip a coin under the rug nearest your front door.

Motivation

64. To summon motivation, enthusiasm, and focus.

*T*his is a quick spell to be performed whenever you are having a hard time concentrating or trying to muster energy and enthusiasm to do something that needs to be done.

In this terse layout, the Ace of Wands depicts pure energy, especially energy directed toward worthwhile projects. The Magician represents you, focusing your attention, applying yourself, and using your energy to create and achieve, and realizing your full potential. The third card can vary, depending on what it is that you need motivation to start or complete. In the diagram, I have used the Eight of Pentacles, which represents work and organization. However, you could substitute other Tarot cards in this position. For example, for help in concentrating on studies, use the High Priestess; to get motivated to start exercising, use Strength; to break a bad habit, use Temperance; to enter a conflict try the Seven of Wands; to summon initiative to leave a bad situation, use the Eight of Cups or the Six of Swords. There are many possibilities. For more help in selecting a card to fit your personal situation, refer to a good book on the meanings of Tarot cards.

The Tarot cards are the only materials you need to perform this spell, since you would most likely want to perform it when there is an urgency to get into or on with whatever it is that needs to be done.

Otherwise, consider using a minimum of accessories—perhaps just a single candle. If you do have time to enhance the layout with other accessories, you may use candles, flowers, crystals and gemstones, and cloth to lay the cards upon in shades or combinations of shades of red for energy, orange for unity of mind and body, yellow for intellect, blue for concentration, green for adaptability, purple for ambition, or white for harmony of all elements.

To perform this spell, you may use it in combination with the ritual in chapter 1, improvise a ritual of your own, or just proceed by laying out the cards and doing the following meditation, visualization, and affirmation.

Meditation and Visualization

First, set the Ace of Wands in place; then stand up. If you are not already standing, stretch every limb, wiggle your fingers and toes, do a few head and neck rolls, and spend a few moments trying to feel your life force as it flows through your body.

Next, set the Magician in place. Picture yourself as the magician in the card. Meditate on the thought that you are a magician with the ability to summon your inner energies to achieve any goal.

Finally, lay down the Eight of Pentacles or whichever card you have chosen to represent what you want to achieve or concentrate on. Spend a few moments thinking about what you want to do, and how you want to do it.

After you have spent sufficient time meditating on the cards and visualizations, carefully, and with as much feeling as you can, recite the following affirmation.

Affirmation

"I summon energy and will,

for great is the power within me!

My life force flows strong

and quickens every cell of my body,

and every atom of my being.

I am energized and refreshed.

My mind is relaxed and calm.

I see clearly and deeply,

and ideas flow easily.

My will is all-powerful.

My body, mind, and spirit are working together

to help me accomplish what I will.

I immerse myself in my work.

I accomplish my goals.

And I am eager to do more and more!"

After saying the affirmation, close your eyes, relax, and put everything out of your mind, including the work that you have to do. Now, count backward from 200 to 0. As you count, you will begin to feel an impulse to stop counting, get up, and immediately immerse yourself in whatever project awaits. However, for best effect, resist these impulses and finish the counting. Then you will be able to get up and get on with your work, feeling enthusiastic and refreshed.

You may consider the spell closed at this point, or you may close it as suggested in the ritual in chapter 1, or as desired.

Obstacles

65. To overcome obstacles presentedby individuals.

*S*ometimes it's hard to make progress when, for various reasons, individuals are placing obstacles in your path. For example, the completion of a project may be unduly hard if your coworkers aren't holding up their end of the job, are refusing to consider new ideas, are bickering among themselves, vying for corporate power, etc. This is a general spell designed to help things go more smoothly when you have to contend with people problems.

This straight layout denotes a smooth path. Strength stands for the strength, endurance, and inner power that you will call upon to face your problems and challenges. The Chariot shows you in control of the situation, on top of your opposition, able to ride roughshod over your problems and plow through your obstacles. The Two of Cups shows the desired outcome: harmony, cooperation, and compromise between essentially opposing viewpoints. *Note*: If you're working this spell in order to deal with a specific person, put his or her Significator underneath the Chariot card. The Chariot is used here as your Significator, and putting it over your opponent's Significator depicts your ability to get him or her moving.)

If you wish to use accessories for this spell, consider candles, flowers, crystals and gemstones, and cloth to lay the cards upon in shades or combinations of shades of white for purity of intention and the harnessing of pure psychic energy, orange for endurance, red for force, green for adaptability, blue for serenity, and brown and black for stubborn strength, rootedness, and immovability (on your part), depending upon which qualities you need to summon for your particular problem.

This spell may be performed at anytime, but you may especially wish to use it when you start to get frustrated over getting nowhere with the people you have to deal with or when you sense that a confrontational situation is developing.

To perform this spell, you may combine it with the ritual in chapter 1, combine it with an improvised ritual of your own, or just proceed by laying out the cards and doing the following meditation, visualization, and affirmation.

Meditation and Visualization

When ready, set Strength in place. Now, contemplate the Strength card, and start to do body movements and exercises that make you aware of the strength and energy flowing in your body. Stretch your body, stretch your limbs, wiggle your fingers and toes, and roll your neck and head; as you do so, strongly visualize and try to feel the life force quickening and circulating through your body with increasing vigor. (You can also do exercises like side bends, fencer's lunges, karate katas, or dance movements.)

After a few moments of stretching and exercising, pause and set down the Chariot. Now stand in place and feel the power you have raised surging through your body, and direct it outward through your arms and hands. With this power, make circular motions with your hands, shaping a ball of white psychic energy in front of you. At this point, visualize in front of you the persons that you are having problems with, and send the ball of energy in their direction. In conjunction with this, do one or all of the following three visualizations, depending on what best meets your needs:

* Picture your problem people being pushed out of the way by the concentration of force you have gathered.

* Imagine yourself as a charioteer, charging forward, with the ball of energy clearing and making smooth the path before you, sweeping all obstacles out of your way.

* Visualize, in detail, the particular situation you have to deal with. Visualize the psychic energy working to sway peoples' behavior and influencing them to be reasonable and cooperative.

Finally, set the Two of Cups in place. Contemplate your particular situation now made ideal, with all parties willing to compromise, cooperate, and reason with each other. Picture your erstwhile opponents as being friendly and helpful.

After you have finished meditating on the cards and visualizations, carefully, and with as much feeling as you can, recite the following affirmation.

Affirmation

"I call upon the power within me
to make smooth the path beneath me!
My energy flows forth
and gently clears the way before me!
By force of personality and force of will,
I calmly push away all energies
that oppose me.
I pass freely through resistance.
I ride easily over obstacles.
I am confident and in control.
And in my wake,
people are transformed.
People are helpful and friendly.
People are easy to get along with.
People value my ideas and are willing to listen.
So it is, and so shall it be!"

You may consider the spell closed at this point, or you may close it as suggested in the rite in chapter 1, or as desired.

Note: To modify this spell for help in overcoming obstacles presented by bureaucracies, follow the directions for the previous spell. However, if the institution you're up against is the government or the military bureaucracy, put the Emperor under the Chariot; if it's the legal system, put Justice under the Chariot; and if it's a school, church, or similar hierarchical institution, use the Hierophant.

Protection

The Chariot

14 Temperance 14

Significator

The Star

66. For protection, defense, and safety.

*T*his is a generalized spell for protection, defense, and safety, including protection of home and safety in travel. It evokes spiritual and supernatural powers to form a shield of protective energy around you and add to your peace of mind and sense of security.

This layout takes the form of a cross, an ancient protective symbol. Your Significator is placed at the center of the cross. If you wish protection for your family as well, place the Ten of Pentacles or Ten of Cups under your Significator. The Four of Wands forms the base, standing for protection in and of your home, which is your haven of refuge. The Chariot forms the top, representing safety in travel and protection in and of your mode of transportation. Temperance and The Star form the arms of the cross. They are both used here to invoke supernatural protection, drawing on the folkloric traditions of guardian angels and watchful stars of guidance.

If you wish to use accessories for this spell, choose candles, flowers, crystals and gemstones, and cloth to lay the cards upon in white to symbolize the shield of pure psychic energy that you will erect around yourself in the course of this spell.

To perform this spell, you may combine it with the ritual in chapter 1, combine it with an improvised ritual of your own, or just proceed by laying out the cards and doing the following meditation, visualization, and affirmation.

Meditation and Visualization

When ready, set your Significator (and the Ten of Cups or Ten of Pentacles, if desired) in place. Consider your reasons for desiring protection. Envision yourself (and your family) in an ideal state of safety, security, and invulnerability, with an invisible force field protecting you.

Next, set the Four of Wands in place below your Significator, as indicated in the diagram opposite. Consider your reasons for wanting your house or dwelling to be protected. Picture your dwelling as secure as a fortress, with an invisible force field around it that no unwelcome intruder can penetrate.

Set the Chariot in place above your Significator. Consider your reasons for wanting your automobile or other modes of transportation protected through all your travels. Visualize your vehicle running smoothly and in perfect condition, with an invisible force field around it, protecting it from all accidents and mishaps. Set Temperance to the left, as indicated in the diagram. Picture a radiant guardian angel leaning over you. You can visualize this angel as being your Higher Self, or as your most idealized image of a protective spirit. Recall any stories you've heard or accounts you've read about spirits interceding to protect people.

Finally, set the Star in place to the right. As you lay down this card, think of all the unseen but powerful and watchful forces at play in the universe around us. Think of these celestial forces acting together to give protection and unexpected help in time of danger or need.

When you have finished the card visualizations, stand up, if you are not already doing so, and assume the "pentagram" position. To achieve this position, stand with arms and legs spread wide, imitating a five-pointed star. (Your head makes the fifth point of the star.) This suggests a medieval alchemical sign representing man made perfect.

Continue to stand in this position while you close your eyes and visualize yourself standing in clear, shallow water under a sky full of stars. The water lapping around you feels cool and pleasant.

As you watch the stars in the sky above, you notice that they seem to be getting closer and closer, until they seem to be whirling in spirals around you. As you watch, you see gold and silver sparks of energy flying out from the whirling stars.

You feel these sparks of energy being drawn to your outspread fingers. You feel it being drawn in through your fingers and through the palms of your hands. You also feel energy coming up through the soles of your feet. You are being filled with and transformed by the power that is drawn through your fingertips, the palms of your hands, your eyes, the soles of your feet, and every pore in your body. You feel this vital force surging through you and radiating outward from your innermost being. It creates a shining white energy field or aura, with flecks of gold and silver in it. You glow like a sun, ever brighter and ever more brilliant.

When the power within you has built to a point of great intensity, hold your two hands in front of you and feel the energy pulsing in your hands. Then, with your hands, shape a globe of pure psychic energy around you. Work from head to toe, front and back, and both sides. Spend as much time as you need, allowing the energy to flow out through your hands. Continue to shape it with circular hand motions and spread it around until it is like a protective eggshell around you.

When you are satisfied with your protective aura, turn your attention to your card layout and make clockwise circular motions over it. Let the energy continue to flow through your hands to reinforce the spell, protecting you as well as your home and your transportation.

When you feel you have done as much as you can toward shaping the protective field of energy around you and around the card layout, carefully recite the following affirmation.

Affirmation

"I call upon the power that is within me
and the power that is around me!
I call upon the sentinels of the heavens!
I call upon all good spirits
and all ministering angels!
I call for protection, defense, and safety!
With white light, a force field
is built around me.
I am shielded and protected at all times.
All negative energies disperse and dissolve
at the touch of the radiant light
that emanates from the core of my being.
All shadows flee.
All harm and danger is neutralized
by the touch of my glowing aura.
By the power within me and the power around me,
only peace, love, and serenity
may exist within my protective boundary!
I am protected.
My family is protected.
My home is protected.
All my modes of transportation and travel are protected.
So it is, and so shall it be!"

You may consider the spell closed at this point, or you may close it as suggested in the rite in chapter 1, or as desired.

✳

Psychism

67. To help develop psychism.

*T*his is a spell to help you develop extrasensory perception and open up channels of higher awareness. The awakening of psychic abilities will give you personal guidance, comfort you with the assurance of spiritual existence, and enable you to see and explore the fabric of the universe.

This layout takes the shape of a crown. As a crown sits atop the head, it symbolizes expanded consciousness, awareness outside the senses, and glory in knowledge.

The Star represents inspiration and guidance from supernatural and cosmic forces. It complements and gives power to the High Priestess, the card of focusing the mind, developing intuition, and listening to inner voices. The Hermit stands for the revelation and interpretation of knowledge. It is used here to aid your understanding of the dreams, visions, and intuitions that will come to you.

As a necessary accessory for this spell, have a candle that will be placed just a few inches beyond the High Priestess card. (Do not light this candle until told to do so.) Plan to lay the cards out on a table where you can pull up a very comfortable chair, so you can be at ease while you do the meditations and visualizations. If you wish to use other accessories for this spell, choose additional candles, or flowers, crystals and gemstones, and cloth to lay the cards upon in shades or combinations of shades of white for concentration of divine light and pure psychic energy, blue for looking inward, and/or purple for psychic experience and spirituality.

It is best to perform this spell either very early in the morning or late in the evening when the world is quiet and you are unlikely to be disturbed. It is good to take a lustral bath beforehand (see appendix 2) and to be dressed magically. For maximum benefit, perform this spell or a shortened version of this spell every day, at the same hour each time.

To perform this spell, you may combine it with the ritual in chapter 1, combine it with an improvised ritual of your own, or just proceed by laying out the cards and doing the following meditation, visualization, and affirmation.

Meditation and Visualization

When ready, light the candle that has been set aside for this purpose. For a duration of between thirty seconds to three minutes, focus on the candle flame, putting everything else out of your mind. For a time between thirty seconds to three minutes, close your eyes and hold the image of the flame in your mind.

After you are through concentrating on the flame, set the Star in place. For a few moments, visualize yourself walking alongside a lake under a star-filled sky. From time to time you pause to dip your feet in the water. Feel the coolness and pleasantness of the water as it laps around your feet. Feel that you are at one with the lake and the land and the stars that glow with ever-increasing intensity in the sky above you. Then, spread your arms outward (both in visualization and in actuality) and say aloud:

"I call upon the wide-ranging powers!
I call upon all good and friendly
spirits of guidance!
Aid me now
in opening my psychic centers!
Help me learn to open myself
to the knowledge
and the guidance
which I seek!"

Next, set the High Priestess in place, as indicated on the diagram. Imagine that you continue to walk along the lakeshore until you come to a temple. The temple will take whatever shape your imagination wants to give it. Visualize yourself going up to the door of the temple. You pull on the doors, but you find them locked. You try again; this time just touching your hand to the door handle. Surprisingly, the door swings wide open. You enter into the foyer of the temple. Now, pause and say out loud:

"I unlock the doors,
I enter the temple,
I go within
I am at one with the secret knowledge.
I see with other eyes.
I hear with other ears.
I feel with other senses."

Now, set the Hermit in place. Envision yourself going deeper into the temple. You pass through several rooms (allow your imagination to furnish them as it desires). Finally you pass through a door into a large but darkened room. Two pillars are standing there—the ones pictured in some versions of the High Priestess card. Between those pillars stands an altar, and on that altar is your candle! You walk up to the candle, hold your hands above it, feeling the warmth of the flame (both in visualization and in actuality) and say:

> "All is made clear
>
> hidden knowledge is brought forth
>
> in the light of understanding."

At this point, visualize that you are no longer in the temple. You have been magically transported back home, and are sitting in your own comfy chair, with the cards and the candle before you.

Now, as you sit quietly, make yourself very aware of your physical body. Then, do the following visualization exercise.

Start expanding your conscious mind outward in a spiral pattern. Start with your body, and make your senses circle around, taking in all the sights and sounds. Scan in an ever-widening spiral, taking in the room that you are sitting in, sweeping through your house, scanning your yard and the street outside, reaching even farther out to take in the houses and buildings of your neighbors, ranging farther still, spiraling through your neighborhood, your town, your country, the world, and outward into space. Then, reverse the process, and bring your consciousness in closer and closer, retracing the spiral until you have pulled back into yourself, sitting in your chair.

At this point, carefully, and with as much feeling as you can, recite the following affirmation.

Affirmation

"I am open and receptive
to higher levels of consciousness.
Spirits of guidance are here for me
and I channel the knowledge they offer.
I am open and receptive.
My psychic centers are quickened.
I open my eyes and ears
to all impressions and intuitions
that are coming to me.
I spread the veil of being
that I may look beyond.
I open the windows of where and when
and I see beyond."

Now, sit back, relax, and let go of all your thoughts. Empty your mind, but open your awareness. Spend several moments waiting to see if any interesting impressions pop into your mind. After you feel enough time has passed, write down any impression you've received. If you feel you haven't received any worthwhile impressions, don't worry—you have started the process in motion, and you'll be surprised to find hunches and insights coming to you at unexpected moments.

If you wish, this is a good time to pursue any other psychic work you're interested in, such as automatic writing, I Ching, casting rune stones, and, of course, Tarot.

When you want to complete your session, you may close the spell simply by extinguishing the candle and putting away the cards, or you may close it as suggested in the rite in chapter 1, or as desired.

✳ ✳

Quarrels

First Significator

Second Significator

68. To stop a quarrel or dispute, and to reconcile opponents.

*T*his is a spell that you most likely would want to use in case two people near and dear to you have been carrying on a long and destructive feud.

In this layout, the cards are set out in a four-quarter cross, representing a balance of all elements. The Significator cards pertaining to the two feuding parties are made to face each other. (If possible, you should position the Significator cards so that the graphic image on the one on the left is facing the one on the right.) The other two cards make the layout self-explanatory. The Two of Cups represents harmony and reconciliation, and it can also represent a dynamic balance—that is, balance and harmony between essentially opposing forces. The Two of Swords is for a truce in quarrels.

If you wish to use accessories for this spell, candles, flowers, crystals and gemstones, and cloth to lay the cards upon can be white to signify purity of actions and motives, and an absence of negative feelings. If you have some pictures of the individuals that this spell concerns, you may have them set up near the card layout. Also, for this spell, place a silver goblet nearby to represent the peace that is desired between the two individuals for whose benefit this spell will be performed.

To perform this spell, you may use the ritual provided in chapter 1, improvise a ritual of your own, or just proceed by laying out the cards and doing the following meditation, visualization, and affirmation.

Meditation and Visualization

Lay out the cards when you come to the appropriate point in the ritual.

First lay down the two Significator cards. Think of the need for these two individuals to resolve their differences.

Next, lay down the Two of Swords, visualizing the figure in the card as a spirit standing between the two antagonists, preventing them from engaging in any more fighting.

Finally, set down the Two of Cups, visualizing the two parties forgetting their old feuds and finding common ground on which to base a friendship. Picture them drinking and laughing together.

After you have finished meditating on the cards and visualizations, carefully, and with as much feeling as you can, recite the following affirmation.

Affirmation

"I call upon all forces for peace and goodness!
Use your powers to end hostilities
and bring reconciliation
between (names of parties)."

At this point, take up the silver cup. Swish your fingers around in the cup and say:

"As I stir the water in this cup
so may feelings of respect and friendship
be stirred in (names)."

Now, let water drip from your fingers onto the Significator cards (but only if your cards are somewhat waterproof), and say:

"May (names)
forget old feuds and quarrels and come together in friendship
working out their differences
and working together toward good and useful ends.
So be it!"

You may consider the spell closed at this point or you may close the spell as suggested in chapter 1, or as desired.

Strength

Your Significicator

1 The Magician 1

The Chariot

Opponent's Significator

69. For help in holding your own in disagreements with a particular person.

*T*his is a spell that you would most likely want to use if you have had a long-standing conflict with a family member, coworker, or other colleague. Perhaps this individual is either a bully or an unusually opinionated sort of person who has a tendency to start arguments, run roughshod over your ideas, or put you down.

The cross-shaped layout for this spell seeks to reset the balance of power in your favor. The opponent's Significator card and the Seven of Wands show the struggle that has gone on before, and the Magician, Strength, and the Chariot show you asserting your strength and wit to hold your own against your antagonist.

If you wish to use accessories in this spell, yellow items of focus such as candles, flowers, crystals and gemstones, and cloth to lay the cards out upon are appropriate. Yellow is the color of mental alertness and will be helpful when you want to emphasize a sharp wit and quick thinking in countering your opponent. On the other hand, if you want to emphasize calm strength and firmness in holding off your opponent, you can use brown accessories, as brown is an earth color suggesting massiveness and immovability. If you can get hold of a picture of your opponent, a strand of hair, or other belonging that has made contact with him or her; this will also be helpful in establishing a psychic connection for this spell.

To perform this spell, you may use the ritual provided in chapter 1, improvise a ritual of your own, or just proceed by laying out the cards and doing the following meditation, visualization, and affirmation.

Meditation and Visualization

Lay out the cards when you come to the appropriate point in the ritual.

First, lay down your own Significator, and then lay the Magician down on top of that. (Unless you ordinarily use the Magician as your Significator, in which case the one card will do.) Picture yourself as having the wit and cunning of a great magician.

Next, lay down your opponent's Significator. Clearly visualize this individual. Think of the conflicts and arguments that you have had. If you have a picture or object belonging to this person, pick it up and handle it at this time. Afterward, it may be stored in a glass jar until the situation improves.

Lay down the Seven of Wands next. Visualize yourself holding your own in an argument with your opponent. Consider how you can manage confrontations in the future by standing up to him or her, not allowing him or her to get to you, making witty quips, rising above the situation, and in general doing whatever it takes to overcome this person's abuse.

Now set out the Strength card. Visualize yourself bathed in a glowing aura, feeling inner power and self-confidence surging through you, knowing that you are indeed ready to meet all challenges.

Finally, put down the Chariot. Visualize yourself as the powerful charioteer, wearing the armor that will protect you from any barbs your opponent may throw at you. Know that you have the strength and ability to keep everything under control.

After you have finished meditating on the cards and visualizations, carefully, and with as much feeling as you can, recite the following affirmation.

Affirmation

"I call upon the power that is within me!

I draw upon strength

and knowledge

and charisma

and self-confidence!

I will hold my own!

I use this power to make myself invulnerable

to the cruel or careless words and actions

of (name of adversary).

I send this power with blessings to (name)

to bring out the good nature within him/her.

When next I meet (name)

I will deflect his/her assaults

I will be calm and in control!

I will rise above all with smiles and radiance.

So be it!"

You may consider the spell closed at this point, or you may close the spell as suggested in chapter 1, or as desired.

✷

Self-Improvement

70. For self-improvement and self-transformation.

*T*his is a spell to assist in bringing about the positive transformation of one's self. It integrates the qualities for both spiritual and physical development.

This layout takes the shape of the six-spoked wheel, a symbol of the union and personal synthesis of all elements. The wheel also symbolizes evolution and progress. And, because a wheel is also a circle, it symbolizes self-analysis, integration, and the completion of the self.

The Magician is in the center of the circle, representing development of potential, and is followed by Temperance, which represents careful management, the Chariot for movement and control, Strength as implied, the High Priestess for looking inward, Judgement for transformation, and the World for completion and fulfillment.

Prior to performing this spell, write on a piece of paper why you feel a need to make improvements, which aspects of your personality need improving, and what course of action you plan to take. When you are ready to perform the spell, lay the cards out on top of this list.

No other accessories are required for this spell. If you do wish to use accessories, decorate your ritual area with white candles, flowers, crystals and gemstones, and cloth to lay the cards upon. White stands for the concentration of Divine Light and the harmonious blending of all colors. As an alternate, you could use accessories of all the colors in the spectrum to create a rainbow effect.

This spell may be performed at anytime, but it is especially suited for days that symbolize new beginnings, such as New Year's Day, your birthday, the first day of the week or month, and so on.

To perform this spell, you may combine it with the ritual provided in chapter 1, combine it with an improvised ritual of your own, or just proceed by laying out the cards and doing the following meditations, visualizations, and affirmations. (Because any person's self-improvement goals are highly individual, the following visualizations and meditations give very generalized suggestions.)

Meditation and Visualization

When ready, set the Magician in place. (You can use the Magician as your Significator, or you can set your Significator underneath it, if you like.) Consider that *you* are a magician because you have the power to use the potentials that life provides you to transform yourself and to create a better life. Visualize yourself shaping your life as you want it.

Next, set Temperance in place, as indicated on the diagram. Think about the ways in which you need to regulate your life. How can you better care for your body and soul? Consider which things in your life need to be set in balance. Visualize your life perfectly managed, with body and soul in harmony with the Life Force.

Next, set the Chariot in place. Are there any new directions you need to take? Think about how you can take control of your life to get things moving. Visualize yourself doing new things and exploring the new directions your life could take.

Set Strength in place, while considering how the qualities of this card are needed in your life. Do you need to build more physical strength? Emotional strength? Spiritual strength? Consider this bit of Eastern philosophy: sometimes strength is found in taking the path of least resistance; leading by effortless effort; controlling by not controlling. Visualize yourself applying these principals to your own life.

Set the High Priestess in place. This is a card of looking inward. What do you need to learn? Know that the wisdom that you've always admired in others is within yourself. Picture yourself calm and serene, able to go within to find your answers.

Set Judgement in place. What sort of changes could you bring about? What sort of attitude changes could result in both physical and spiritual transformations? Picture yourself making these changes and becoming a person who is superior in every way.

Finally, set the World in place and contemplate what it means to be a totally integrated person, in harmony with the world around you. Picture yourself enjoying success, full health, and happiness.

After you have completed these meditations, spread both of your hands over the Magician, and draw them apart slowly, making a circular motion over all of the cards. Feel that white light is drawn from all of the cards; sense that you are shaping it into a soft velvety ball of light between your hands. You shape it as you sense the light growing stronger and stronger, the globe becoming thicker and thicker.

Now, transfer the power into yourself by bringing your hands up over your head and spreading them all over your body, while sensing that you are drawing the power within. You take in all of the qualities that you have visualized, and then some!

After you have finished visualizing the transfer of psychic energy into your being, carefully, and with as much feeling as you can, recite the following affirmation.

Affirmation

"I am the best person that I can be!
I take control of the circumstances that affect me
and that are a part of my life.
I shape them so that the greatest good results.
I master all things because my will is strong.
I take care of the needs of my body and soul.
I look within me
to find serenity
and knowledge.
I move in the directions I want to go in
and I make the transformations I desire.
All is whole within me.
All is complete within me.
I live in balance with the world around me.
And my world reflects my inner harmony."

You may consider the spell closed at this point, or you may close the spell as suggested in the rite in chapter 1, or as desired.

Stress

71. For releasing stress.

*S*tress lies at the root of many, if not most, of the problems we suffer from today. Stress plagues us as individuals as well as a society. This spell will help you learn to ease your stress by helping you release anxieties, obligations, and guilt.

The essence of this layout is releasing fears and cares, giving yourself over to the Higher Powers, knowing that you are cared for, and accepting that things will work out for you. The shape of the layout mirrors the "tau" cross in the Hanged Man.

The positive interpretation of the Hanged Man applies to periods of time in your life when it is necessary to pause and withdraw from activities in order to reconsider attitudes, goals, and lifestyle. It advises you to step outside of your usual routine and set time aside for rest, relaxation, recuperation, and reflection. The Hanged Man also signifies letting worries go by putting your faith in a Higher Being or Power. The Four of Cups, Temperance, and Ace of Cups all reinforce this advice, respectively representing a reevaluation of your situation and your priorities, setting your life in balance, and seeking emotional refreshment and spiritual nourishment.

We give you a choice of three alternate actions to accompany the affirmations in this spell; you can choose the action that is most convenient for you, depending on where you are when you feel a need to perform it. The first action requires no accessories. The others respectively require either a length of cord or string which should be at least one foot long, or a beaded necklace. The beads do not have to be uniform; they can be of differing shapes and sizes.

If you wish to use other accessories for this spell, use candles, flowers, crystals and gemstones, and cloth to lay the cards upon, in shades or combinations of shades of cool colors such as blue, green, and lavender. Blues represent serenity and calm, greens represent refreshment and adaptability, and light violet represents spiritual reflection.

When you have a stressful situation that is an ongoing thing, such as a high-pressure job or a perpetually tense family situation, it is a good idea to set some time aside to perform this spell each day (especially if you are suffering from hypertension or other stress-related ailments).

This spell can also come in handy when unexpectedly stressful events interrupt your normal routine. When that happens, perform this spell or an abbreviation of it, depending on how much time you have available. If you are in the middle of a tense situation and have only a few moments, just say the affirmation, or just perform the action with the cord or the necklace while you think the affirmation.

To perform this spell, you may combine it with the ritual provided in chapter 1, combine it with an improvised ritual of your own, or just proceed by laying out the cards and doing the following meditation, visualization, and affirmation.

Meditation and Visualization

When ready, set the Four of Cups in place. Consider how changes in action and attitude could ease some of your stress. Are there obligations that you can cancel or postpone? Or are there emotions from which you need to separate yourself? Perhaps you are putting pressure on yourself when you feel that your ego is on the line.

Set Temperance in place and ask yourself whether you can make concessions and compromises to strike a balance between the obligations that you must take care of, even though they may be stressful, and the activities that give you pleasure and contentment. Open your awareness to the life force of the universe; let its healing energy flow through you like a river. As water finds its own level, being in this flow will help you find equilibrium.

Put down the Ace of Cups. Promise yourself some rewards. What sort of activities, hobbies, or other treats will refresh you? What will give you spiritual and emotional enrichment?

Finally, set the Hanged Man in place as indicated in the diagram. Study the picture on the card. Look at the serenity in the face of the hanging figure. Understand that by submitting your cares to the Higher Power, however your religion or personal philosophy perceives it to be, you will be taken care of. Suspend your anxieties; worrying is not productive. Know that there is a Divine Plan for you. Allow the life force to flow freely, and everything will work for your highest good.

After you have meditated on the cards, do one of the three following exercises to release tension.

* While holding the symbolism of the Hanged Man in your mind, take ten deep breaths while you try to make yourself more relaxed. If you are in a place where you are able to do so, lay down, bending one of your legs and leaving the other straight, in imitation of the figure in the card. Close your eyes and visualize yourself floating in space, suspended between heaven and Earth. Imagine the gentle cosmic winds

blowing around you and through you, purging you and bearing away all of your anxieties. All the while, breathe deeply and feel yourself getting more and more relaxed. Relax and let go. Feel your heart beating slowly and easily, and reach serenity by easing tension throughout your body, releasing emotions and worries that are no longer needed. When you feel that you are relaxed as much as you can be, count from 200 backwards to 1, then continue this spell by saying the affirmation provided. *Note:* Counting backward from 200 works well if you're overwrought and don't have the other materials or the affirmations available. Relax as much as you can, close your eyes, and count, knowing that the very act of counting is relaxing and relieving you more.)

* Take a length of cord and tie it in eighteen knots. Then say the affirmation provided, untying a knot after each line of the affirmation.

* Take a necklace, and starting at one bead or one point on the necklace, finger each bead in turn. As you rub the beads, say the affirmation provided. With each line of the affirmation, hold a different bead between your fingers, feeling its shape and texture. If you finish the affirmation before you finish counting the beads, just repeat a few of the more meaningful lines from the affirmation until you've come back to the point from which you started.

Affirmation

"I am relaxed and serene.
I am at peace with myself.
I forgive all errors.
I release all guilt and sorrow
to flow away from me
like leaves carried away by a stream.
I am secure.
I am nourished by the living universe.
I give myself over to the Higher Powers
and suspend my cares
outside of time,
outside of space.
All experience is unfolding as it should.
Everything falls into order.
and in the fullness of time
all is taken care of.
Everything works for my highest good,
and everything works out for me."

You may consider the spell closed at this point, or you may close the spell as suggested in the rite in chapter 1, or as desired.

Throughout the days that follow, when you get a chance, rerun the spell in your mind to inculcate the antidote for stress into your own psyche: being at peace, being at ease, being relaxed.

✳

Theft

Thief's Significator

Justice

Your Significator

72. To recover stolen property.

*T*his is a spell to help you recover money or belongings that have been stolen. The layout shows the forces of justice being summoned to compel the thief to release what is not his or hers, and to see that the stolen property is returned to you.

The Seven of Swords can be quite literally interpreted as a theft or "rip-off," just as its picture seems to indicate. This card is reversed to show that the thief will not be able to hold onto what he or she has taken. If the identity of the thief is known to you, select a Significator for him or her and place it under the Seven of Swords. (Refer to appendix 1 for choosing Significators.) Justice is an auspicious card that stands for the powers that enforce justice, whether they be worldly or otherworldly agencies. The Ace of Pentacles stands for wealth coming in, and here represents your own goods or cash being returned to you. To reinforce the idea of the goods being returned to you, place your Significator under the Ace of Pentacles.

Notice the flow of the graphic symbolism in this layout: the sword of Justice is held up toward the thief, while the judge's scales are lowered to the Ace of Pentacles, suggesting that your goods will be handed back.

This spell will require burning a special candle each day for nine days, so obtain nine red candles. Here, red is used to symbolize force and immediate action. If the name of the thief is known to you, inscribe the name or at least the initials on each of the candles. Make a list of the items that have been stolen, and each day set a new candle on top of this list. Do not light the special candles until instructed to do so at the appropriate point in the spell.

If, by some chance, you have something belonging to the thief, have this at hand when you perform the spell. Any police reports or other information or evidence pertaining to the theft can be kept on hand, too. Also, if you have some items that had been in close physical contact with the stolen items, you can set them near the card layout to affect a magnetic pull on the missing items. Also, have a sharp, preferably two-edged, knife on hand.

If you wish to use other accessories to enhance the card layout area, you can use additional candles and flowers, crystals and gemstones, and cloth to lay the cards upon in shades or combinations of shades of red for action, green for money, gold for attraction, and white for purity of motive and pure psychic energy.

After you have established that a theft has taken place, plan to work this spell at a time of the day when you will not be disturbed, and perform this spell at the same time each day for nine days.

To perform this spell, you may combine it with the ritual provided in chapter 1, combine it with an improvised ritual of your own, or just proceed by laying out the cards and doing the following meditation, visualization, and affirmation.

Meditation and Visualization

When ready, set the thief's Significator in place, if you have one for him or her, and set the Seven of Swords immediately on top of it. (If you do not have a special Significator, the Seven of Swords will be enough.)

Think about the theft, and go over what you know about the theft in your mind. Think of the thief, if you know who it is. Form a strong picture of him or her in your mind. If you have anything that belongs to the thief, pick it up at this time, and stroke it slowly and carefully several times.

Take up the knife and point it at the Seven of Swords. Strongly visualize the thief being tortured by mysterious stabbing pangs. (If you do not know who the thief is, just picture him or her as a figure in shadow.) Picture the thief coming to the realization that he or she will get no rest until that which was wrongfully taken is returned.

Next, set Justice in place as indicated in the diagram. Picture a stern and angry judge. Know that you don't have to specify who this judge will be—it can be the law, any divine forces or ministering spirits that aid the just and the oppressed, or, indeed, it could be the thief's own conscience. Picture the judge telling the thief that he or she has done wrong, and he or she must make this situation right by returning the stolen items.

Finally, set your Significator in place and set the Ace of Pentacles immediately on top of it. Picture yourself receiving back the stolen items. Do not qualify how these items will be brought back; they may be brought back through the law enforcement agencies, they may be returned anonymously by the thief who has felt compelled to make things right, or they may come back to you through various other means or channels. If you have any items that had been in close contact with the stolen items, pick them up and stroke them several times.

Sense how elated you will feel to have the recovered property back in your own hands. Envision yourself feeling very good that everything has been made right.

After you have spent sufficient time meditating on the cards and visualizations, take one of the special large red candles you have prepared, set it on top of your list of stolen items, and light it. Then, carefully, and with as much feeling as you can, recite the following affirmation.

Affirmation

"I call upon the fundamental justice
which pervades all things!
I call upon the forces of the universe
which do decree and enforce this justice.
Powerful forces are set in motion,
and my property is returned to me!
The thief (name if known) is compelled
to give up that which is mine.
The thief feels nothing but pain and torment
until my property is returned.
The thief (name) is compelled
by the forces of the law.
The thief (name) is compelled
by forces of conscience.
The thief (name) is compelled
by forces unseen.
Everything is returned to me.
Everything is mine again.
All is well!
So it is, and so shall it be!"

You may consider the spell closed until the next day at the same time, or you may close it as suggested in the ritual in chapter 1, or as desired.

When you have completed the spell, do not think about your stolen property until you perform the spell again the next day.

Allow the candle to burn out. Repeat this spell every day until all of the nine candles have been burned down.

✶ ✳

Appendix I
Choosing a Significator

When the layout for a spell calls for a "Significator," "your card," "his or her card," or "subject," it will be necessary to insert an appropriate card to describe either yourself or another person in question. Significators can also be used for groups, institutions, or organizations.

When selecting a Significator card to represent yourself or another person, you can use the list of cards suggested below, or any other card than you feel is the most descriptive. In some cases you might use a card that represents the ideal you—the person you wish to become.

The Fool. A child or adolescent, an innocent or inexperienced person, "Everyman," an adventurer or traveler, an individual who needs to make a decision, an individual who is about to embark on some kind of venture.

The Magician. A person becoming aware of his or her potential, an ideal man, a sorcerer, an engineer or someone in the applied sciences, an artist or artisan.

The High Priestess. A person trying to get in touch with his or her self, an ideal woman or dream woman, an individual who holds a secret, a psychic, a wise woman, a scholar or researcher, a research scientist; also initiatory orders.

The Empress. A woman of authority, wealth, and power; a pregnant woman, a mother or Earth mother, a female political figure.

The Emperor. A man of authority, wealth, and power; a father or father figure; a male political figure; a military or law enforcement officer, a captain of industry. Also the government, a corporation, the military-industrial complex.

The Hierophant. A teacher or mentor, a member of the clergy, someone concerned with ceremony or hierarchy; also a religious or educational institution, a ceremonial order.

The Lovers. A couple.

The Chariot. Messenger, a person involved in transportation, military personnel.

Strength. A forceful person, a courageous person, an athlete.

The Hermit. A seeker of knowledge, an elderly person, a person looking into the past, a guide, a recluse.

Justice. A person who must weigh a decision; someone involved in law or law enforcement; an arbitrator; also the legal system and law enforcement organizations.

The Hanged Man. A person who feels his or her life is in stasis; a person who has voluntarily retreated from work-a-day life to devote himself or herself to meditation and reflection; a patient in a hospital; a martyr.

Temperance. A healer, a manager, a disciplined person, a resourceful person, a conservationist, a protective spirit.

The Devil. An extremely negative or destructive person.

The Star. Someone who offers unexpected help, a muse, a deeply spiritual or inspired person, a very beautiful person, an artist, an entertainer, a celebrity.

The Sun. A child or children, a celebrity, an artist or creative person.

The World. A self-actualized and fulfilled person; a dancer, a naturalist.

Two of Wands. Business partners.

Three of Wands. A person involved in commerce; also a corporation.

Five of Wands. Competitors, a competitive group, a sports team.

Six of Wands. A victorious person.

Seven of Wands. A person engaged in a struggle, a person holding his or her own against opposition, a visionary.

Nine of Wands. A defensive person; also military personnel.

Ten of Wands. A laborer, a heavily burdened person, an overworked person; also a labor union.

Page of Wands. A youth who is active, gregarious, enterprising, and adventurous; someone who takes on employment at an early age; a messenger; if reversed, a gossip or loud mouth.

Knight of Wands. A person who is involved in and involves others in new projects, directions, and adventures; when reversed, a seducer, a risk taker, a person whose energies are scattered.

Queen of Wands. A businesswoman; a "take-charge" sort of woman; a woman involved in lots of activities and projects; an entrepreneur; if reversed, a seductress.

King of Wands. A businessman; a "take-charge" sort of man; a man involved in lots of activities and projects; an entrepreneur; if reversed, a man who neglects responsibilities.

Two of Cups. A couple, partners.

Three of Cups. A social club, a circle of friends, a celebrational community.

Four of Cups. A person who is bored with a peaceful but static emotional life; a person who is reevaluating his or her situation.

Five of Cups. An emotionally restless person, a risk taker; a person suffering from burnout; an embittered person.

Six of Cups. Children, childhood friends.

Nine of Cups. A person who has and enjoys luxury, a generous host, a person who overindulges.

Ten of Cups: A family, a family-like group.

Page of Cups. A youth who is sensitive, imaginative, affectionate, emotional, and dependent; if reversed: an emotionally disturbed child, a child of divorce.

Knight of Cups. A lover; one who brings love into the subject's life; an attractive, romantic, idealistic person; if reversed: an unfaithful lover, an unreliable person.

Queen of Cups. A woman with strong feelings, emotions, dreams, visions, and religious ideals; an attractive woman; an understanding, empathetic woman; a nurse; a caretaker, a social worker; a woman who loves animals; if reversed: a woman who is masochistic or over emotional.

King of Cups. A man who is warm, loving, sensitive, religious, poetic, and idealistic; a member of the clergy; a social worker; a man who loves animals; if reversed: a man who is unreliable, unstable, and unfaithful; a weak man.

Four of Swords. A person recuperating from an illness; a person on a retreat.

Seven of Swords. A very clever person, a thief; a person who is "getting away with something."

Eight of Swords. A person who feels trapped by circumstances.

Nine of Swords. A person with many worries and anxieties.

Page of Swords. A precocious youth; if reversed: a sneaky or manipulative child, a delinquent.

Knight of Swords. A person who is intellectual, assertive, and brave; a person who is involved in or involves you in a conflict; if reversed, a person who gets you in trouble.

Queen of Swords. A woman who is intelligent, perceptive, and analytical; a woman who has the power to fight on your behalf; a military woman; a lawyer; a professor; if reversed: a ruthless and vindictive opponent, a woman corrupted by power.

King of Swords. A man who is intelligent, perceptive, and analytical; a man who has the power to fight on your behalf; a military man; a lawyer; a professor; if reversed: a ruthless and vindictive opponent, a man corrupted by power.

Two of Pentacles. A person who must juggle a lot of duties and obligations.

Four of Pentacles. A homeowner, a wealthy person, a miser; also a bank or financial institution.

Six of Pentacles: A philanthropist; also a service club or charitable institution.

Seven of Pentacles. A farmer, an investor, a planner; also an agricultural concern.

Eight of Pentacles. A worker, a craftsperson; also a labor union.

Nine of Pentacles. A self-sufficient person; a person who is able to work out of his or her home.

Ten of Pentacles. A family, a dynasty.

Page of Pentacles. A youth who is studious, conscientious, and responsible; if reversed, a very stubborn child.

Knight of Pentacles. A single person who is reliable, stable, hard-working, prudent and conservative; reversed: a person who could entangle you in bad debts; an unhelpful civil servant.

Queen of Pentacles. A woman who is gracious, refined, socially conscious, trustworthy, conservative, and financially secure; a matriarch, a patron of the arts; if reversed: a woman of reduced circumstances, a stingy and suspicious woman.

King of Pentacles. A man who is responsible, trustworthy, cautious, conservative, a good money manager; a man concerned with appearances, a patriarch; a patron of the arts; if reversed: a man who has suffered severe financial setbacks, a man who is stingy and suspicious, an unreasonable bureaucrat.

Appendix II
Preparation for Spells and Rituals

*I*n order to purify the body and set the mind in the proper attitude, certain simple preparations are advised prior to a magic working.

Diet. An individual should avoid eating heavy meals prior to magical workings, simply to avoid sluggishness. Some persons prefer to fast for a certain amount of time prior to performing a spell or rite, and others choose to do without certain foods such as meat, stimulants like coffee, or depressants like alcohol. Dietary restrictions are, however, a matter of personal choice.

The Lustral Bath. A bath of purification is desirable prior to any special working. Such a bath is usually taken by candlelight, and the bath water itself is often sprinkled with sea salt and fragrant herbs. While one is in the bath, the mind should always dwell on the thought that the water is washing away all impurities of the heart, mind, and soul.

Clothing. Clothing and jewelry that help you feel beautiful and magical are ideal for working magic. When performing a spell, choose clothes that make you feel that you are stepping outside of your mundane reality. The only requirement for clothing is that it be loose enough to allow you to move and breathe freely and easily.

Workspace. For the purpose of the spells in this book, be sure that you have an uncluttered surface where you can lay out the Tarot cards and any extra accessories you may want. Also, magical workings are best performed in areas that are free of distraction, congenial in appearance, and freshly cleaned. When spells and rites are regularly performed in a special place, the area seems to "come alive" in both obvious and subtle ways. Even those who are only slightly sensitive psychically will soon observe that there is a definite "charge" or aura about the vicinity.

Appendix III
Accessories for Spells: Tools for Magic

A number of spells in this book suggest the use of accessories other than the basic Tarot cards. (A few spells require specific accessories, though in order to keep the spells as simple as possible most accessories are just optional.) You will find such items to be helpful in focusing your spells. Also, by taking the extra time and effort to enhance and personalize your spells with accessories, your magic will be intensified as more psychic energy is directed to your goal.

The following list provides some additional information on the use of these articles in magic. It gives a little background for these magical tools, with the exception of candles, crystals and gemstones, and color correspondences, which are treated in appendices IV, V, and VI respectively.

Braziers. A brazier is a large, wide-mouthed bowl (it can be a large incense burner) which is fireproof and can be used for burning small things such as bits of paper. A brazier is called for in two of the spells in this book that involve the purging of negative emotions. The negative thoughts are written down on paper, which is then burned in a brazier to achieve purification by fire.

Cloth for Card Layouts. Some piece of cloth (it can be a tablecloth, runner, place mat, handkerchief, doily, etc.) can be used as an optional accessory to lay the Tarot cards out on. Such a cloth helps the eye define and focus on your work area, and is best if it is of a color that enhances the purpose of the spell. (Color associations are given in the individual spells, as well as in appendix VI.)

Coins. Coins are used as accessories for some of the money and business spells, and their symbolism is obvious. The treatment of the coins in these spells is based on the occult principle that like attracts like. In the Tarot, coins are symbolic of the Earth powers, as some Tarot decks use "Coins" instead of "Pentacles" in the suit of the Minor Arcana which represents abundance, security, stability, diligence, attainment, and efforts rewarded.

Cups. Cups are used for performing certain symbolic actions and gestures in some of the spells in this book. In Tarot symbolism, cups represent the magical virtues of the element of water, which governs love, pleasure, happiness, beauty, emotions, relationships, fellowship, healing, and spiritual and emotional sustenance. As symbols of receptiveness, cups are also images of the unconscious mind and its connection with dreams and psychic and intuitive functions. In some of the spells concerning divorce, family concerns, friends and quarrels, cups are used to represent harmonious relationships. In a few spells concerning dreams and psychism, a cup is used to symbolize the deep mind.

Flowers. Flowers are very appropriate as accessories to grace your magical work area. Aside from setting a pleasing mood, they have their own elemental vitality and lend energy to a spell. It really isn't necessary to choose any particular variety of flowers, but it would be a nice touch to use flowers whose colors are coordinated with the purpose of the spell. (Color associations are given in the individual spells, as well as in appendix VI.)

Incense. When doing a magical working, the burning of incense creates an atmosphere that helps us feel that we are stepping outside the mundane world. It is also an ancient belief that the smoke carries thoughts and prayers upward to the heavens. I believe that any incense whose fragrance is pleasing to you is quite suitable for any spell you want to do. However, if you want to get more deeply involved with it, there are many excellent books that describe different types of incense blends and their traditional magical uses; occult shops and catalogs also sell incense packaged for special spells. I don't insist on the use of incense with the Tarot spells, because people with smoke allergies may be bothered by it. If you do want to light incense, you'll also need a metal or ceramic incense burner, brazier, bowl, ashtray, or cup with sand in the bottom to absorb the heat. Briquettes of self-igniting charcoal are also especially useful for the burning of incense.

Knives. As magical tools, knives correspond to the Minor Arcana suit of Swords. Most Tarot systems ascribe to knives and swords the elemental powers of air, whose properties include intellect, wit, communication, quests, protection, courage, force, aggression, and law. In many magical systems, knives (often called athames) are used to direct the individual's inner power outwards. This book doesn't really require knives as magical accessories. Rather, the spells that direct you to send power outward explain how you can do it by visualizing power flowing through your hands and fingers. A knife is used in the spell for discouraging enemies and pests in order to bring pressure to bear, and also calls upon the folkloric symbolism of the knife, which is severance of ties.

Mirrors. Mirrors are used in some of the beauty spells, as they symbolize pride in physical beauty. They are set up to reflect multiple images of the Tarot cards, which are the images of the ideal that you are striving for. A full-length mirror is called for in some health spells in order to facilitate whole-body awareness. In addition, mirrors have long been used in folk magic, where they represent such symbolic lunar qualities of mystery, unconscious knowledge, and imagination. In some traditions mirrors are thought to be windows or portals into other dimensions.

Personal Items, Photos, and Pictures. Personal items, photos, and pictures help you hold in your mind a sharper image of your subject. Personal items—objects belonging to or linked with other persons may be called for in spells intended to influence another person. It is especially desirable to have such an object present when a spell is being performed on behalf of a person who can't be present. There is also a very ancient belief in "sympathetic magic," based on the idea that things touched or used by a person take on some of that person's essence, and if you perform symbolic acts on the person's belongings, you can psychically affect him or her. In some of the spells in this book, you will be instructed to handle the personal objects (if you have them) in certain ways in order to create a stronger link. In spells aimed at influencing other people, there is of course a question of ethics, so it is assumed you will have read the section on ethics in chapter 1. In some cases, you may want to affect institutions or organizations, in which case photos would probably give you the best link. Certain types of pictures are also called for in spells where you need to focus on idealized images.

Strings, Cords, and Necklaces. The spell for dealing with stress gives you options including tying and untying knots in a string or cord, or counting the beads on a necklace while you say the affirmation. In this case, these things are merely used for simple but effective relaxation exercises. However, tying knots while saying a spell has played a part in folk magic, and cords used for this purpose are sometimes called "witches' ladders." Necklaces also have significance because they symbolize unity, wholeness, and the cycle of life.

Water. Water is used in some of the spells in this book. In some cases, such as health spells, symbolic washing is done for bodily purification and awareness; while in other spells, water or another liquid is imbued with power to create a magical elixir. Water is symbolically associated with the deep mind, as well as with spiritual sustenance.

Writing. The written word has power, and writing can be a magical act. Some of the spells herein require you to make lists or write things down for various reasons. In a number of ancient and primitive societies, writing was viewed as a mystical art. Many letters may have originated as magical sigils. I once heard a psychiatrist say that he requires patients to write down resolutions when trying to modify habits or make self-improvements because the act of writing actually engages more sections of the brain, thereby reinforcing the person's resolve. One can see how this would also heighten and direct magical energy.

Appendix IV
Candles

*T*here are a few spells in this book that require the burning of candles, but for most of the spells candles are optional, albeit highly recommended, accessories. Candles have the obvious advantage of providing a pleasant way to illuminate your card layout area, but they also have magical significance. Fire has its own vitality, so its use lends energy to a spell. The noted occultist Dion Fortune felt that fire emanates etheric substance. Candle burning also evokes a primitive fascination with the power of fire to purify and to ward off evil. Because fire is also synonymous with light, it symbolizes spiritual illumination and helps us tune into higher states of consciousness.

Due to the magical as well as symbolic importance of fire, candle burning has long been a vehicle for working magical spells. Candles are a very popular tool for practitioners of folk magic, many of whom draw upon some very ancient traditions. The use of ritual and votive candles to accompany prayer and worship in many of the world's religions is in itself a form of magic. Some very effective magical systems have been developed around candle spells. Raymond Buckland's book *Practical Candle-burning Rituals* offers a very comprehensive treatment of candle magic, and is a good source for anyone wishing to look deeper into this practice.

Preparation of Candles

Because the Tarot layouts are the foundation of the spells in this book, and because the spells are designed to be as simple as possible, no special type of candles or preparation of candles is required. However, if you are able to take the extra time to "dress" your candles, you will boost the energy and sharpen the focus of your spells.

To dress a candle, you anoint it with oil. You can just pour a little oil onto your fingertips, then rub them over the candle, starting at about the middle and working outward to both ends. As you anoint the candle, think about the magical goal that you are working on. Complete the dressing by covering the wick and the bottom of the candle as well.

Any varieties of scented oils that you can obtain in crafts shops are quite suitable for candle dressing. If you wish to be more particular, occult shops and catalogs do sell specialty oils meant for use with love spells, money spells, and others.

Incidentally, the size, shape, and type of candles to be used don't really matter. Use whatever is convenient. It is a good idea to use candles of the colors recommended for use with the accessories for the individual spells. (Refer to individual spells, as well as appendix VI, "Color Symbolism.")

After you have closed a Tarot spell, having done the visualizations, affirmations, etc., you can allow your candles to burn down, or you can snuff them out, depending upon convenience and preference. If you are putting full concentration into a very specific magical working, you might want to allow any candles used to burn down completely, thereby adding to the spells' sense of completion and closure. On the other hand, if you are working specific spells or a series of spells daily or on a regular basis, using the various spells as part of an ongoing process to better your general situation in life, then you may want to put the candles out at the end of each session. You would use and reuse the candles in the course of numerous regular sessions.

(*Note:* Some feel it is better to snuff a candle rather than to blow it out. Breath symbolizes life, and is therefore seen as inappropriate for extinguishment.)

Appendix V
Crystals and Gemstones

Crystals and gemstones have long been believed to possess mystical properties, and they have their own special place in magical lore.

Currently there is an increase in the popularity of these beautiful stones. Use of crystal power is often the first thing that comes to many people's minds when they think of the various trends that are components of the New Age.

The type of crystals that are most popular and are generally the ones referred to in New Age literature are the clear quartz crystals. Quartz crystals have the familiar crystal shape terminating in a point with six facets. Such crystals have a strong appeal, whether you prefer them natural (with raw points), or polished and shaped. There is also a growing interest in other gemstones, including colored varieties of quartz such as amethyst, and gems that do not have the familiar crystalline shape. These can include rough stones as well as those that are polished and cut for use in jewelry.

Proponents of crystal power recommend them for such various uses as meditation, the release of stress, achieving inner peace, health and healing, dreaming, improving mental acuity, protection, divination, channeling, and the sharpening of all psychic faculties.

Some psychics believe crystals have innate magical properties, and that the alignment of the crystal structure with the Earth's electromagnetic field lends it the ability to store and channel psychic energy. Those who believe in the paranormal powers of crystals point to their physical properties. Due to the precision of the molecular structure of crystals, they store electrical energy. If you squeeze a crystal, it will build up an electrical charge. Crystals have important applications in the electronics industry, in which their electrical oscillations are used for frequency standards, ultrahigh-precision clocks, and specialized optics. Thus, because crystals are regularly used in industry to generate and control electrical energy, those who accept the possibility of mental and psychic energy also believe crystals have magical applications.

Others would argue that the power of crystals is psychological, and that perhaps the magic of the crystals is not in their structure, but in their beauty. These "flowers of the Earth" have an aesthetic appeal that sets a magical mood and helps us focus our thoughts for meditation and more sublime states of consciousness.

At any rate, crystals can be used as a "key" to bring the unconscious mind into focus and trigger its paranormal capacities.

Crystal enthusiasts are also not in total agreement on which forms of crystals are the best. Some prefer raw crystals, but try to choose those with more neatly shaped points, while others who also like raw crystals say the quality of the points doesn't matter. There are also crystal users who have a preference for stones that have been polished and shaped.

Because the body of information and lore of crystals is quite massive and is continuing to grow as more people find new applications for crystal power, I cannot effectively treat this subject in depth here. I recommend that those wishing to learn more about crystals and gems read some of the popular books on the subject, including *Crystal Awareness* by Catherine Bowman, *Healing with Gemstones and Crystals* by Diane Stein, *Crystal Healing: The Next Step* by Phyllis Galde, and *Cunningham's Encyclopedia of Crystal, Gem & Metal Magic* by Scott Cunningham.

Use of Crystals in Tarot Spells

For the purposes of these Tarot spells, crystals and gemstones are optional accessories, to be used only if you have them available and want to include them. If you want to use them to enhance your spells by holding and amplifying the power you raise, you needn't know any of their lore nor have any previous experience with them. You can simply place crystals, gems, and other appealing stones around your card layout area in aesthetic arrangements. The stones you use do not need to be of any particular variety, but you may want to choose stones coordinated to the colors recommended for use with accessories for the individual spells. (Refer to the individual spells, as well as appendix VI, "Color Symbolism.")

If you do use crystals or other gemstones as accessories to step up the power of your Tarot card spells, select the individual stones that you find you have a particular affinity for. It's a good idea to obtain five of them—one for each corner of your card-layout area (north, east, south, and west); and your largest and/or best one to be placed directly upon your focal card or Significator as you complete your affirmation. Alternately, the fifth or "power focus" stone may be placed at the center of your layout area. Whatever approach you take, be sure that it's the one that "feels right" to you personally. Then, proceed as directed for the individual spell.

Before you use your crystals or gemstones in a spell or for other magical or psychic purposes, you might want to get them tuned up by going through the following preparation.

Preparation of Power Crystals

Note: For the following preparational instructions, the term "crystal" is used, as crystals are so popular. However, if you have some unidentified stones that do not appear to have a crystalline structure, but which you would still like to use for magical purposes, you can substitute the word "stone" wherever the word "crystal" appears.

When you first obtain some crystals or gemstones that you feel can be useful, it is advisable to purify and charge them before you use them. At the time of the new Moon, wash the stones thoroughly in fresh, cold water, saying:

> "Cleansed are these crystals.
> Purged of all residual energies
> and undesirable influences.
> Only the good, the pure,
> and the strong remain herein.
> These crystals are now made receptive
> to the powers
> that I shall instill within them.
> So may it be!"

Then allow the crystals to dry thoroughly. On the following day, or as soon as is practical, take the crystals out into the bright sunlight. Take a matchbox or small wooden box and put in enough fresh, clean salt to completely bury the crystals. Then place your crystals in the salt and work them back and forth with your fingers, holding the open salt box out in the sunlight and saying:

"At this time and at this place
is the great power of the Sun
drawn within this box,
within this salt,
within these crystals.
Strength and life are affixed
within each of these living,
crystalline minerals.
The power grows
and makes them ever stronger,
drawing from the great Sun itself.
And by the Sun . . . so be it!"

If it is possible, leave the saltbox out in the bright sunlight for a few minutes or more to build the charge higher. What feels right to you is important here.

It is a good idea to have the crystals packed in cotton within their own jewelry case when they are not being used, and to have them stored near your bed when you are sleeping.

Reusing the Crystals

After you have closed a Tarot spell, you can set your crystals in a safe place where they will remain undisturbed until you're satisfied that your magical goal has been reached. If the purpose of the spell is to help you with personal matters such as love, employment, self improvement, etc., you can carry the crystals on your person or keep them where you can see and handle them every day in order to draw upon their energy.

When your goals have been reached, you can reuse the crystals for new spells. It is also a good idea to renew the cleansing and/or the solar charging given in the power crystal preparation after you have finished performing one spell and before you start the next. Fresh, new salt should be utilized each time you perform this rite. (After the first purification and charging, it is not necessary to wait for the new Moon to perform this rite. Your needs, rather than the time of the month, are more important.)

If you are working specific spells or a series of spells daily or on a regular basis, using the various spells as part of an ongoing process to better your general situation in life, then you do not need to recharge the crystals each time. You can allow their power to build and grow through the course of numerous regular magical sessions.

Appendix VI
Color Symbolism

To enhance each spell, various colors have been suggested for any accessories that may be desired: candles, flowers, gemstones, cloth to set the card layouts on, etc. Colors help create focus for a spell by setting a mood and evoking emotional responses. Some medical researchers find that different colors do affect our nervous systems differently. Also, some psychologists suggest that colors have a traditional symbolism that affects us through our cultural conditioning.

Use of color may also lend extra power to a spell. Many occultists believe that colors have subtle vibrations that have a magical effect of their own.

The following list provides the color associations that are used with the spells in this book. Although each spell has a section that suggests the best colors to use, you may wish to refer to this list for extra information. This symbolism is drawn from Western cultural traditions, some Eastern traditions, psychology, and magical theory.

Red. Energy, vital force, enthusiasm, activity, impulse, immediate action, human love, passion, sexuality, eroticism, conception, child bearing, and childbirth.

Pink, Rose. Affection, warm feelings, feeling good, well-being. This is the color assigned to music faculties in American colleges.

Red, Violet. Ambition, noble actions.

Purple, Violet. Spirituality, psychism, creativity, inspiration, dignity, authority, high stations in life, nobility, generosity. This is the color worn by law faculties in American colleges.

Blue, Violet, Indigo. Spiritual reflection, meditation, intuition.

Blue. Peace, serenity, relaxation, honesty, fidelity, understanding, introspection, concentration, patience. This is the color of philosophy faculties in American colleges.

Light Blue. Sincerity, loyalty, devotion.

Green. Nature, the freedom of nature, youth, growth, fertility, resilience, adaptation, regeneration, physical and emotional healing, the color of medical faculties in American colleges, opportunity, prosperity, money, financial security, comfort, the Druidic color of knowledge.

Yellow. Happiness, cheer, hopefulness, intellect, alertness, wit, wisdom, science, confidence, communication.

Orange. Warmth, energy, vitality, focused energy, action directed by intellect, unity of mind and body, persuasion, endurance. This is the color assigned to engineering faculties in American colleges.

Gold. Radiance, charisma, attractiveness, expansiveness, wealth.

Silver. Charm, mystique, purity of understanding.

White. Purification, purity of intentions, psychic energy, spiritual strength, purified emotions and absence of negative feeling, unity and harmony (because it is the result of all the colors in the spectrum combined).

Black and White Combination. The Cabbalistic colors of knowledge, black representing understanding because it absorbs all light, and white representing the quintessence of Divine Light.

Black. Total concentration, impenetrability, protection, immovability, firm and somber resolve, absence of light.

Brown. The Earth powers, strength rooted in the Earth, a simple lifestyle, security, stubborn strength.

Appendix VII
Responses to Commonly Asked Questions

Can I customize spells?

Yes, you can adapt the spells by changing some of the words and images. You can also design new ones: pick out Tarot cards whose images relate to what you want to achieve, then arrange them in a way that tells a picture story of what you would like to see happen, while affirming or praying for what you want. If you cannot find Tarot cards that picture the things you want, you can substitute photos, drawings, cutouts, or cards with your desires written down on them. Add any other touches that feel right to you. There is no wrong way of performing any of these spells, and everything can be adapted to suit your own needs and individuality.

What do I do if I can't find a spell for what I want?

The spells in *Tarot Spells* are necessarily very general. It was not possible to provide a spell for every situation that a person may need to deal with, so refer to the previous question on customizing spells.

Can I do spells for other people?

Yes, if you have the consent of the other person, you can improvise by altering words and visualizations, and making other changes as you see fit, or as suggested above.

Can I perform more than one spell at a time?

Yes, you can do as many spells as is comfortable and convenient. Look at it this way: there is no reason why a person couldn't say as many positive affirmations as he or she wanted, and a spell is another form of affirmation.

How many times should I repeat a spell?

Unless otherwise indicated, it is probably not necessary to perform any spell more than once, though you may repeat a spell as often as you wish, if this boosts your confidence, or if you enjoy the magical experience. Bear in mind, too, that sometimes it may look like nothing is happening, but there could be things happening on deeper levels, which may take their own time in manifesting.

What will happen if I don't perform a spell correctly?

Don't worry about whether you performed a spell correctly. The Tarot spells are designed to direct psychic energy toward goals, but these methods are not etched in stone. The important thing is whether you are able to create an experience that enables you to step outside the boundaries of ordinary existence and signal your desires to the Higher Powers.

Will my spell work?

With the spells provided in *Tarot Spells,* or any other spell book, you must realize that spells proclaim your desires to the cosmic powers and set spiritual energies in motion, but they can't always guarantee success because there are so many other factors that come into play. It's the same with magic as with anything else: you can do all the right things to start a certain kind of business or grow certain kinds of plants, but whether your business or your gardening is a success may depend on a lot of other things, including things that you have no control over. Remember, on page 2, I say that magic involves "nudging probabilities," but sometimes the probabilities may not be in your favor. Or, as I say in *Playful Magic*: sometimes there are too many negatives, too many outside factors and variables, or too many other forces aligned against a magical objective, thereby reducing the probabilities involved . . . desperation and negative emotions can also work against magic by acting as negative affirmations. And of course, if we accept the idea that there are some greater destinies that we may not always be aware of, then some things are just not meant to be. However, the number one obstacle to magical success is cross-purposes, that is, when you have two conflicting issues. That is most likely to occur when the different facets of your personality have motivations that do not run parallel to each other.

How long will it take for my spell to work?

This question cannot be answered. As previously mentioned, not all spells work, and the fact that many different variables affect any given situation makes it impossible to know which ones will work and how long they will take.

Are there any drawbacks or negative consequences to performing Tarot spells?

The spells in my book are all positive in tone and deal with good energies. It is conceivable that some persons could adapt the principles in *Tarot Spells* for use with things of a more negative nature, in which case they might experience some problems since negative thinking tends to attract bad luck. If you have additional ethical concerns about performing the spells, (for example, if you fear that receiving a new job or a promotion may displace someone else), you can end the spell by saying, "I have performed this spell in the sincere belief that my desires are in keeping with God's will [or with the harmony of the Living Universe], and I accept that all things will work out for my good and the good of all other persons involved. If this is not meant to be, I accept that in the knowledge that something even better is in store for me." Also, love spells can be bad medicine when they involve attracting or hanging on to someone who is wrong for you. Here is the problem: because that certain combination of factors we call "chemistry," as well as mutual respect, maturity, and the ability to handle responsibility and commitment are so important to any relationship, if you feel the need to do a love spell on someone, chances are that person is probably wrong for you to begin with. If you cast an ill-considered love spell, the object of your spell may agree to marry you—or whatever—but you may be miserable in the long run, because you've gotten stuck with someone who is bad for you. Think very carefully before performing a love spell. Most of the people who ask me about love spells would be much better off if they took up some sport, hobby, or other enterprise that would build their confidence (thus making them more attractive to the opposite sex) and would also take them out into the world where they could meet a larger variety of people (thus increasing their chances of meeting Mr. or Ms. "Right").

Should spells be kept secret?

Generally, whether you want to keep a spell secret or not is up to you, and depends a lot upon your personal circumstances. Discussing positive spells with people that you can trust will not diffuse the power of the spell—it may increase it in some cases, by bringing your friends into a greater understanding and sympathy with your goals. On the other hand, it would be better not to discuss spells with persons who may be unsympathetic, resentful, or who might misunderstand your actions or motives.

Could you use your powers and perform a spell for me?

I do not lay claim to any special powers, and for various reasons do not do spells for other people—not even for money. I wrote *Tarot Spells* and *Playful Magic* to empower people by showing them how to do their own spells.

Are you going to write any more books?

In addition to *Tarot Spells*, I have written *Playful Magic*, and *Tarot: Your Everyday Guide*, which is about how to use Tarot cards to get advice on courses of action for common situations. I am now working on *Tarot for Teens*.

Bibliography

In concluding, I hope that this book will help you to see life magically, and to better develop a sense of your own inner power in influencing the world around you.

If you would like to know more about using practical magic to enhance daily life, a wide variety of books on this subject are available. The range of techniques and methods is quite extensive. Some worthwhile books that provide spells as well as different approaches to practical magic include:

Buckland, Ray. *Advanced Candle Magic.* St. Paul, MN: Llewellyn, 1996.

———. *Practical Candleburning Rituals.* St. Paul, MN: Llewellyn, 1971.

———. *Practical Color Magic.* St. Paul, MN: Llewellyn, 1983.

Cunningham, Scott. *Earth Power: Techniques of Natural Magic.* St. Paul, MN: Llewellyn Publications, 1983.

———. *Encyclopedia of Crystal, Gem and Metal Magic.* St. Paul, MN: Llewellyn Publications, 1987.

———. *Magical Herbalism: The Secret Craft of the Wise.* St. Paul, MN: Llewellyn Publications, 1982.

Cunningham, Scott, and David Harrington. *The Magical Household.* St. Paul, MN: Llewellyn Publications, 1987.

Denning, Melita, and Osborne Phillips. *Practical Guide to Creative Visualization.* St. Paul, MN: Llewellyn Publications, 1980, 2000.

Grimaud, B.P. *Tarot of Marseilles.* Paris, 1969.

Malbrough, Ray. *Charms, Spells, & Formulas.* St. Paul, MN: Llewellyn, 1990.

Morrison, Dorothy. *Everyday Magic: Spells & Rituals for Modern Living.* St. Paul, MN: Llewellyn, 1998.

Ravenwolf, Silver. *Teen Witch.* St. Paul, MN: Llewellyn, 1999.

———. *To Light a Sacred Flame.* St. Paul, MN: Llewellyn, 1999.

Telesco, Patricia. *Spinning Spells, Weaving Wonders.* Freedom, CA: The Growing Press, 1996.

Worth, Valerie, *The Crone's Book of Magical Words.* St. Paul, MN: Llewellyn Publications, 1971, 1986, 1999.

Also, if you would like to know more about the meaning and magic of the Tarot, the following books offer different explanations, insights, and applications:

Butler, Bill. *Dictionary of the Tarot.* New York: Schocken Books, 1975.

Clarson, Laura G. *Tarot Unveiled: The Method to Its Magic.* Stamford, CT: U.S. Games Systems, 1988.

Echols, Signe E., Robert Mueller, and Sandra A. Thompson. *Spiritual Tarot: Seventy-Eight Paths to Personal Development.* New York: Avon, 1996.

Gettings, Fred. *The Book of Tarot.* London, England: Triune Books, 1973.

Gray, Eden. *The Tarot Revealed: A Modern Guide to Reading the Tarot Cards.* New York: Bell.

Greer, Mary K. *Tarot for Yourself—A Workbook for Personal Transformation.* North Hollywood, CA: Newcastle, 1984.

Hamaker-Zondag, Karen. *Tarot as a Way of Life: A Jungian Approach to the Tarot.* York Beach, Maine: Weiser, 1997.

Jayanti, Amber. *Living the Tarot.* St. Paul, MN: Llewellyn, 1993.

Kaplan, Stuart R. *Tarot Classic.* New York: Grosset & Dunlap, 1972.

Louis, Anthony. *Tarot Plain and Simple.* St. Paul, MN: Llewellyn, 1996.

Pollack, Rachel. *Seventy-Eight Degrees of Wisdom.* London: Thorsons-HarperCollins, 1997.

Reed, Ellen Cannon. *The Witches Tarot.* St. Paul, MN: Llewellyn, 1989.

Free Catalog

Get the latest information on our body, mind, and spirit products! To receive a **free** copy of Llewellyn's consumer catalog, *New Worlds of Mind & Spirit,* simply call 1-877-NEW-WRLD or visit our website at www.llewellyn.com and click on *New Worlds.*

☽ LLEWELLYN ORDERING INFORMATION

Order Online:
Visit our website at www.llewellyn.com, select your books, and order them on our secure server.

Order by Phone:
- Call toll-free within the U.S. at 1-877-NEW-WRLD (1-877-639-9753). Call toll-free within Canada at 1-866-NEW-WRLD (1-866-639-9753)
- We accept VISA, MasterCard, and American Express

Order by Mail:
Send the full price of your order (MN residents add 6.5% sales tax) in U.S. funds, plus postage & handling to:

Llewellyn Worldwide
2143 Wooddale Drive, Dept. 978-0-87542-670-9
Woodbury, MN 55125-2989

Postage & Handling:

Standard (U.S., Mexico, & Canada). If your order is:
    $24.99 and under, add $3.00
    $25.00 and over, FREE STANDARD SHIPPING

AK, HI, PR: $15.00 for one book plus $1.00 for each additional book.

International Orders (airmail only):
    $16.00 for one book plus $3.00 for each additional book

Orders are processed within 2 business days.
Please allow for normal shipping time. Postage and handling rates subject to change.

Tarot: Your Everyday Guide
Practical Problem Solving and Everyday Advice

JANINA RENÉE

Whenever people begin to read the Tarot, they inevitably find themselves asking the cards, "What should I do about such-and-such situation?" Yet there is little information available on how to get those answers from the cards.

Reading the Tarot for advice requires a different approach than reading for prediction, so the card descriptions in *Tarot: Your Everyday Guide* are adapted accordingly. You interpret a card in terms of things that you can do, and the central figure in the card, which usually represents the querent, models what ought to be done.

This book is especially concerned with practical matters, applying the Tarot's advice to common problems and situations that many people are concerned about, such as whether to say "yes" or "no" to an offer, whether or not to become involved in some cause or conflict, choosing between job and educational options, starting or ending relationships, and dealing with difficult people.

1-56718-565-7
312 pp., 7½ x 9⅛ $12.95

To order, call 1-877-NEW WRLD
Prices subject to change without notice